DON'T

I Can't

Forget the Critics

Unlock your Millions

"Donna Rae is the epitome of drive, dedication, determination and a living example of one of my favorite lines, It's Possible"

Les Brown

Melanie —
Ask. Believe.
Receive !

Donna Rae

First published by Busybird Publishing 2018
Copyright © 2018 Donna Rae

ISBN
Print: 978-1-925830-95-8
Ebook: 978-1-925830-28-6

Cover design: Busybird Publishing
Layout and typesetting: Busybird Publishing
Editor: Allison Duncan

Busybird Publishing
2/118 Para Road
Montmorency, Victoria
Australia 3094
www.busybird.com.au

Testimonials

From the time she was my student in a high school English class, Donna has been a driven individual. As her passion for public service and business ownership grew, she capitalized on her talent to be heard. She always transforms her ideas into bigger and better real world solutions. As the owner of several small businesses and as an elected public official, Donna speaks from those experiences to motivate others to do the same.

> **Jane Blystone, Ph.D.**
> **Retired Director of Graduate Studies in Secondary Education**
> **Mercyhurst University, PA**

What sets Donna apart from others is her tenacity. In my mind, that will be her legacy as a school board member. She effectively blended a demanding, yet supportive role, that helped our District regain its recognition as one of the premier school districts in the state of Pennsylvania. Her tireless efforts and advocacy will be difficult to replace.

> **William Hall, Superintendent**
> **Millcreek Township School District**

Dedication

To my boys, Ryan and Shane; I owe my sincerest gratitude that you not only tolerated me but encouraged me during both my darkest and brightest days. To see your successes is truly a mothers' blessing.

And to my sister DeeDee; I miss you every day, but I also know that you have been by my side through the heavens encouraging me to keep talking!

And finally, sincere thanks to anyone who ever told me that I couldn't do something.

I just did!

Contents

Forewords i

   Change Your Thinking - Change Your Life iii

   Get Focused v

1. Finding Your Why 1

2. Being Tenacious 11

3. Unlocking Shortcuts 23

4. Mentors to Millions 35

5. Sell It! 47

6. Fail to Win 59

7. Niche 71

8. Network Equals Net Worth 79

9. Overcoming Roadblocks 89

10. Changing Direction 101

11. Living Your Best Life 113

12. Tenfold Returns 125

About the Author 137

Forewords

Change Your Thinking – Change Your Life

*D*onna Rae is a true champion of success. Her inspirational life story caught my attention years ago and I am thrilled to lend my support to this great piece of work.

Don't Tell Me I Can't speaks of Donna's stubbornness to live and not die; to rise above challenges instead of conceding, while snatching victory from the jaws of defeat.

For parents or business owners alike, *Don't Tell Me I Can't* is a practical resource that we can all relate to, but more importantly, Donna is transparent; exposing her flaws, through her bravery and tenacity, it's clear.

If Donna can do it, I can too!

As a busy mother with major health challenges, Donna still did not give up. She had every reason to let life collapse around her; she had every reason to quit … she did not.

In fact, her advice is simple: life is going to come with obstacles. Don't let it be the end of your world. Change your thinking, and it will change your life.

Let me share a secret with you: don't ever tell Donna Rae she can't! She is the epitome of drive, dedication, and determination, and a living example of one of my favorite lines: *it's possible.* *Don't Tell Me I Can't* will change your mindset and reprogram your thinking for success.

Get out of your head and into your greatness.

Live your dreams,

Les Brown

www.lesbrown.com

Get Focused

I will start out this foreword by warning you, dear reader, of the power you now hold in your hands! This book does not only educate, but will also create a defining moment on how a person can go from one adversity to another, and come out clean. For too long we have led ourselves to believe that our current situations will be our ultimate destinations.

Well, no more!

Donna Rae has brought to light the grim truth about staying in a negative state of mind for too long. This is a book about overcoming adversity and it does not sell its reader short. I'm serious:, this is a great book and I've learned some really powerful things from it.

Let's talk about the author for a moment. Donna Rae is a phenomenal woman. She has the heart of a child but the will of a warrior. She knows a thing or two about going through adversity and relocating to start anew. Donna is someone who understands that the world is not all sunshine and rainbows, but she seems to walk around with her own personal rainbow maker.

Honestly, I have seen life rain all around Donna, yet in her mind, and evidenced by her behavior, Donna has found a way to live upon the beautiful energy of a rainbow.

When others get tired, Donna gets focused. When others complain, Donna moves forward. The author is truly an expert at this subject.

This book will help you think about your dream and envision your future. Regardless of the disappointment you have faced while pursing your dream, this book will remind you that your dream is not dead.

Most people don't move past adversity, they settle within it. They build houses and plant gardens in adversity, and it never goes away because hardship was never designed to just disappear.

In life, adversity doesn't disappear; the strength in people appears. This book will help you set goals that will stretch and bring out the best you.

Donna Rae understands that there will never be a perfect time to move past adversity. This book teaches its reader that now is the only time to get past tough times. Donna has written a book about growth; a book that won't give you permission to be average. This book will help you find the reason why you should get back up and find out where you are supposed to be, and it will encourage you to make the sacrifices needed to make your dreams a reality.

Lastly, dear reader, this book will challenge you more than you want. It will force you to get from the low levels of life and reach the highest expression of yourself.

It won't let you get comfortable with what you did last week, it will only allow you to focus on your present power and greatness. Donna Rae has written a masterpiece, which is not surprising because she herself is a masterpiece.

You can plant better, you can dominate.

Antonio T. Smith, Jr.
www.theatsjr.com

1
Finding Your Why

*H*ave you ever been asked the question, what is your *why?* What is it that gives you the drive to get out of bed each day and make the absolute most of every day? Once you have that figured out, you will unlock unlimited potential in your life, both professionally and personally.

According to a Wealth Research Group report, 98% of people die without achieving their why (*Why 98% of People Die Without Fulfilling Their Dreams*, July 17, 2016, http://wealthresearchgroup.com). I would say that by age ten I had my *why* figured out.

Our mother raised us that if we wanted something, then we had the ability to go out and earn it. Nothing was for free. I'm not talking about earning money doing chores around the house – that was expected. Each year the highlight of our summer would be the cherry festival, which was hosted by our volunteer fire department. I knew that there were four days of absolute fun, games, rides and a bunch of junk food to offer. In order for me to be able to attend the cherry festival with my friends, I had to make the money ahead of time. There's nothing like learning how to budget at ten years old.

Our parents would give us the opportunity to go out and earn as much money as we desired on the farm. Make no mistake though, if you chose not to go out and work the hours prior to that festival, there were no loans being given.

I used to joke with my parents as an adult that I should have turned them in for violating child labor laws, but they were quick to remind me that if it's your own child, those laws don't apply. My *why* was starting to cultivate at a very young age on the farm, as I was being taught the very life lessons that I didn't even know were part of my parents' plan. I was starting to see that I appreciated what I had more than some of my friends did, because it wasn't given to me. I had to work for it and I earned everything I had.

My *why* was becoming clearer by the day. I knew that no matter what, no matter how many people told me that I couldn't do something, I was going to continually set goals and do everything that I needed to do to achieve them. British journalist Walter Bagehot may have summed it up best, "A great pleasure in life is doing what people say you cannot do." You must always remember, too, that it doesn't matter what other people think of your *why*, the reasons that you choose to do things are your reasons.

My *why* has come from a mixture of things. As a kid, I wanted to make my mother proud. As a teen, I found out that my competitive side was part of my *why* also. I simply didn't want to lose. As I transitioned into my adult years, it became more about what I could do for others. As I continued to set and achieve goals, I had resources available to me that I was now able to share with others.

Your *why* can not only change your life for the better, but also the lives that you touch. Without a *why* your life can be a very empty one. It is very important to have the mindset of all the reasons you can do something. If you tend to focus on all the reasons why not, reaching your goals is going to become more than problematic.

Mindset is everything. We have 12,000 to 60,000 negative thoughts a day. Keep in mind, your brain is one of the most powerful organs in the body. You as an individual have the ability to change the direction of your thinking. In the best-selling book *The Secret*, the author Rhonda Byrne continually talks about how thoughts become things. Have you ever got out of bed one morning and it seemed that everything was going wrong? One bad thing snowballed into a day full of bad things. It may be that you've talked yourself into the notion that it was just going to be a bad day.

One morning I had a very important conference to attend. First, I slept through my alarm and after getting out of the shower, I pulled my hairdryer out and it wasn't working. The frustration level was increasing rapidly. Then I remembered the words in *The Secret*. Thoughts become things. I was unnecessarily amplifying everything negative that was happening to me. I took a deep breath and I literally said out loud, "Slow down." So my hair wasn't going to be exactly the way I planned for it to be that day.

I thought to myself, is that a reason to let my day be ruined? I reprogrammed my brain to get rid of the negative thoughts and thought more about how amazing the day was going to be. Coincidentally, during the conference, I received a phone call. Our company, General Exterminating, was chosen to participate in the ABC network's *Extreme Home Makeover*. Not only were we going to get to participate in the makeover, we were going to be part of the press conference to kick off the makeover. You can't buy that kind of advertising. I firmly believe that if I had not changed the direction of my thoughts that morning, this opportunity would never have presented itself.

If you know what your purpose in life is, you will be unstoppable. Your *why* in life is your purpose. Make finding your purpose a priority. I recently read a quote from Jon Gordon's *The Power of Positive Leadership* (John Wiley & Sons, 2017): "We don't get burned out because of what we do, we get burned out because we forgot why we do it."

I certainly had times where my purpose was being challenged, where I was feeling a bit lost. During those times I would lack energy, enthusiasm and focus. Face it – in every life there's going to be negative outside influences. During the times that I was feeling stuck and questioning my own purpose, I chose to look for outside help.

One of the most critical times in my life was when I was going through a divorce from my husband who is also my business partner. Our behavior during that time would not only affect our livelihoods, but the livelihoods of the people who worked for us. I sought the outside help of a psychiatrist. Why do they refer to psychiatrists as shrinks? Because they help you reduce your problems. Ask for help not because you are weak, but because you are strong.

The more that you know what your purpose is, the less chance you'll have of allowing outside distractions to get you off course. Knowing your *why* is what inspires you to take action. Your *why* statement should be able to be summed up in one sentence and should apply to both your personal and your work life.

Friedrich Nietzsche once said, "He who has a why to live for can bear almost any how."

If you're unclear what your why or your purpose is, you need to take a look at a few simple things. What is it that makes you come alive when you get out of bed in the morning? Do you have something that really excites you? Or do you just go through the motions day in and day out? What are your strengths, and do you use your strengths to add value to your day or to somebody else's? And one of my favorite lessons that I used to teach my kids was, "If you don't stand for something, you'll fall for anything."

You also have to have a clear definition of what success means to you. For some people, paying the rent on time is considered a success. It's not that they don't get out of bed and daydream about a more fulfilling life, it's that they have yet to find what their purpose in life truly is and are simply going through the motions.

Every good company has a solid mission statement. A mission statement helps to determine the direction the company is going. It's also designed to focus on the future and it provides a framework of how to bring all these things together. Your purpose should be your mission statement. I bet if you asked some of the most successful entrepreneurs what their *why* is, it has nothing to do with money. In the early stages of my first business, I did go to work each day, focusing on how much money I was going to make. It didn't take me long to realize that my focus should not be on the amount of money I was making, but rather how I was going to best serve the needs of the clients: without clients, there is no money.

It was difficult for me at first, because I wasn't in a glamorous business. I was in the pest control industry. When people would call asking for help, it was because they were typically at their tipping point when dealing with an insect infestation. By the time the call came into our family business, it was likely that they had called several of our national competitors and they were simply shopping for price. I quickly realized that if I took the time to listen to their concerns as well as explain a solution, then I was giving them much more than the cost to do a job. I was adding value that my competition wasn't.

I was now excited, and my focus shifted from it being all about me to being about our clients. You may be able to guess what happened as a result. That's right, we were growing and making more money.

The purpose I had in my professional life was now allowing me more time with my sons Ryan and Shane, as well as the financial resources to do just about anything that our hearts desired. I was no longer focusing on what I had to do as much as what I wanted to do. While I loved my career, nothing compared to the time that I was able to spend with my boys. The key to life should be spending less time on the unimportant things and more time on the things that we love. I was finally worrying much less about society's expectations of me and working towards the expectations that I had for myself.

Not too long ago, while packing for my move to Florida, I came across the eulogy that I had written for my mother's funeral. It included the poem *The Dash*, by Linda Ellis. The poem starts out, "I read of a man who stood to speak at a funeral of a friend. He referred to the dates on the tombstone from the beginning…to the end." The poem highlights that the important part of the tombstone is the dash – the part between the beginning and the end. My mother had lived such a fulfilling life, it was clear to me that she knew her purpose and that she lived each day intent on fulfilling her purpose. Losing my mother was one of the hardest times of my life, but knowing that she lived her *why* was something to celebrate, not mourn.

If you were to die today, is your life one worth celebrating too?

If you even had to think about how to answer that question, then it's time that you start making a conscious effort on how to improve yourself. Fear is the number one thing holding people back from living their dreams. Fear makes you question everything and act on nothing. Fear encourages you stay in an uncomfortable situation, simply because it's a familiar one. This is the reason that people stay in careers they're not happy with, or refuse to leave abusive relationships. Fear holds you back, rather than expands who you are.

If you don't choose a path for yourself, a path will be chosen for you. Too often we choose the path of least resistance. Some people literally have a fear of being successful. Society is sending mixed messages, that somehow being successful is a bad thing. Also, there's fear of the unknown. Would you rather live your life paralyzed by fear and living in a daydream? Or would you rather start each day with a passion to live your purpose? Once you commit to living your dreams, you're going to be amazed to find out that everything you needed was always within your reach. Everything that you once thought to be impossible suddenly becomes possible. You will no longer be focusing on the reasons why not, and the word *can't* will no longer be part of your vocabulary. Mediocrity will not be an option. You will begin to see humor in the things that you once feared. Your happiness is something that you're no longer wishing for, but rather waking up to each and every morning.

Yesterday I received a call from my nephew, Rocky. He was concerned, because each morning he would start his day by reading my inspirational quote of the day on Facebook and that for a few days in a row, there were no posts made. He was worried that something might be wrong. I told him that

I started those posts during a time when I was struggling myself, and I did it because I knew that if I started each and every day with gratitude, it would set the pace for my day. You can't imagine how overwhelmingly happy I was to find out that I was making a difference in somebody else's life with a daily ritual that I started to improve my own.

Rocky would be the first to admit to you that there was a period of time that no matter how positive things were, he would find the negative side of it. I can't tell you how pleased I was to learn that my nephew has found his purpose, which is helping to propel him into success beyond his imagination.

2
Being Tenacious

*A*re you seeking rapid results?

If you are, then I suggest that you find your tenacious side. We all have one. Many confuse being tenacious with being arrogant. Tenacity, however, is working smarter, not harder. In the words of Amelia Earhart, "The most difficult thing is the decision to act, the rest is merely tenacity."

Being tenacious means you are persistent in seeking what you value, determined to achieve what you desire.

Your tenacity could potentially overwhelm others, and you could be judged as being pretentious or overbearing. But tenacious people are simply those who put their eye on their target and do what needs to be done to achieve it.

There is a saying, "Don't judge someone by how many times they have been knocked down; judge them by how many times they get back up." Persistent people will do what's needed to get things done.

You may be wondering how you find that tenacious side. For me, my tenacious side comes from wanting something badly enough that I will do anything to achieve it. And of course, being told that I can't do something definitely increases my tenacity.

A line from business coach Art Petty stuck with me. He said, "Tenacity is one of those common attributes of most successful people. It's often one of the key missing ingredients of chronic underachievers." Have you ever known someone who can look at and identify countless reasons why someone else is unsuccessful, yet they're struggling to get by themselves? I've known more than my fair share. I'm not suggesting for a moment that these people lack intelligence or are even lazy. As a matter of fact, a *Fortune Magazine* article from January 2016 suggested that nearly 70% of our adult population have not only the talent to succeed, but great ideas to go along with their talents. What's lacking is the tenacious side that makes them want to get out and put action behind their words. You could be the best coach and cheerleader on the planet, but until a person decides that they want something badly enough for themselves, their circumstance will never change.

I remember back when my children were young, they played highly competitive hockey. There was always that one kid who stood out with amazing talent, yet they didn't use it to the best of their abilities. As frustrating as it would be, I remember telling my sons that you can teach somebody how to play a game, but you can't teach them heart.

One of my favorite books of all time is *It's Not Over Until You Win* by my favorite author, Les Brown (Simon & Schuster, 1997). At first glance, I thought, what a catchy title for somebody who can't stand losing. I think my favorite part of the book is when Les Brown talks about how he arrived at this very title. He goes onto explain about how one night he was playing countless games of Connect 4 with his son John

Leslie. After winning multiple games in a row, he told his son it was time to call it a night. But John Leslie was not going to let him off the hook that easily. He responded to his dad, "It's not over until I win." His tenacity was not going to allow him to go to bed without winning. He kept at it, changing his strategy until he was able to win.

It is that kind of desire to win attitude that will take you far in life. I'm not quite sure at what point society decided that raising kids to be competitive was somehow going to be detrimental to their futures. I remember back when James Harrison of the Pittsburgh Steelers sent out a tweet that said, "I came home to find my boys received trophies for nothing. Participation trophies. While I am very proud of my boys for everything they do and will encourage them till the day that I die, these trophies will be given back until they earn a real trophy." Choosing whether you want to go through life just participating versus competing will certainly contribute to the outcome of your career. We cannot allow apathy to take over and accept that "good enough" is welcome if we want more out of life.

I remember on occasion leaving ice rinks where my boys would complain that they didn't get equal ice time. Their dad and I were very much on the same page in pointing out that if they didn't have equal ice time, it's likely because they didn't put forth an equal effort either in practice or at crunch time. The head scout for the Tampa Bay Lightning, Jake Goertzen, wrote that tenacity is crucial to success. Even people who lack talent and fail to cultivate some of the other vital qualities of a team player have a chance to contribute to the team and help it succeed if they possess a tenacious spirit.

I probably shouldn't share this example of how I taught my boys another lesson in tenacity. My boys, like most brothers, would often start wrestling around for fun. It didn't matter that I would tell them to settle down, they would continue until one of them would end up in tears. I got tired of being the bad guy having to discipline the winner, so I started taking a new approach. I told them that if they were going to be wrestling around, then the first kid to cry would be the one who would be grounded. I never saw tears again. Neither wanted to lose, but if they did, they had to take full responsibility for it and were not allowed to run to their mom to protect them. They are now adults and partners in business. That lesson in tenacity as kids is certainly paying off today.

Steven Mariboldi summed it up in the simplest of terms in *Unapologetically You: Reflections on Life and the Human Experience* (A Better Today, 2013). He said, "The only thing that makes life unfair is the delusion that it should be fair." It took me well into my adult years and running a business to realize that the lessons that our parents taught us on the farm as young children were actually shaping us into better and more productive adults. I often joke that my tenacious side came from being the youngest of nine who lived on a farm that had only one shower and that shower was on a well. You didn't want to be last in line because there was no guarantee that there would even be water left for you. Our upbringing taught us that if we wanted something bad enough, hard work and determination would make it possible.

Your success in life is going to be contingent on whether you can turn your ideas into actions; or will you be part of the 70% club who simply talk about what they want to do? In order to produce rapid results, you need to have mental toughness. It is imperative to always maintain the mindset that you are in control. It's not wise nor recommended to waste your time on things that you cannot control, and don't waste your time trying to change others.

You must always set clear goals followed with an action plan on how you intend to accomplish those goals. Les Brown inspired me with a story that is very fitting for this chapter. To keep himself inspired, he would listen to motivational speakers and read their books every chance he had. He shared with us that one of the most powerful speakers that he had listened to was Robert Schuller. He decided one day that he was going to set the goal to be a guest on Robert Schuller's radio show. There was only one big hurdle. He didn't know Robert Schuller, nor anybody else who knew Robert Schuller. He did what any tenacious person was going to do, and he started asking everybody he met if they knew him. He'd ask the person in line next to him at the grocery store, or the guy at the gas pump, "Do you know Robert Schuller?" As you may have guessed, his tenacity paid off. He actually met somebody who didn't know Robert Schuller directly, but knew somebody who did. It was his relentless desire and action behind it that would lead to Robert Schuller calling him personally to invite him as a guest on his show.

If you're still struggling to find your tenacious side, start spending time with other tenacious personalities, the kind of people that through encouragement take you to a higher level of doing things. Hard work alone will never guarantee success. I know many people who work their tails off for several hours each week but are still struggling. In order to speed up your success, you need to be willing to step outside of your comfort zone and take chances.

This is one area where my business partner and I were definitely at odds. He preferred the slow persistent approach, where he did things methodically. I, on the other hand, was ready to change things as often and as much as I needed to, to bring about change in a positive direction.

There were many times when we were at an impasse. I had to remind him that times were changing rapidly, and if you weren't willing to change with the times, then you were increasing the probability of becoming a statistic: another family-owned business who went out of business due to reluctance to change.

As I developed in business, I learned to live by the saying, "Say yes now and worry about it later." A tenacious person will never turn down an opportunity. The persistent person may not turn down the opportunity, but they want to take time to think about what the outcomes could be before making the commitment. But in order to speed up and increase any result, it starts with one simple word, and that word is "yes".

Several years ago, our small family-owned pest control company was given the opportunity to bid on a very large termite pretreatment. We were given a very short window of time to submit the proposal. When my partner and I looked at the specifications, he was more than reluctant to submitting a bid. Our company was in growth mode, and me being the numbers side of the business, I was very excited about what being awarded this bid could do for our bottom line that year. This was a perfect example of "say yes now and figure it out later."

My partner was concerned that we would not be able to keep up with the demand of the project while tending to our own regular customers. He finally agreed that we could submit the bid, but he was doing it assuming that we would never be awarded the bid because the larger chain companies were going to be more competitive price-wise. Lo and behold, we were awarded the job. Now we were forced to put together a strategy on how we were going to manage all this additional work while lacking the financial resources to hire new people and buy new equipment.

The average person utilizes a small percentage of their brain's ability, but when the brain is engaged, activity actually increases. We had no choice but to put our brains together and fulfill the commitment that was made. To this day, over twenty years later, that remains the single highest paying job on our books. Being tenacious means giving all that you have, not more than you have.

There are ways to improve your tenacious side. First, quit watching the clock. I have yet to meet a successful person who was content by punching in at nine and punching out at five. Or those who set a daily quota on sales and when that quota is met, they call it a day. The most successful people that I know are starting their day with enthusiasm long before anyone else arrives, and end their day long after everyone else has left. If you are already working these long hours and not yielding the results that you expect from it, then you must evaluate how those hours are being spent and design them to be more efficient.

You must separate yourself from anything that is distracting you from your goals. Look at your day. How many hours are being consumed by things that are not driving you towards a more successful life? While social media is key today in promoting just about anything, the wasted time spent browsing is time that should be spent working towards your goals. In addition, the amount of negative clutter on social media can be a bigger distraction than you may realize.

What are you making more of, excuses or money? If the answer is not money, then you need to take a deep look at the reasons that you have not made a tenacious attempt to achieve your dreams.

You have to be willing to sacrifice things that seem important to you at times.

I would have loved nothing more than to be a stay-at-home mother, but that meant I would have to delay my financial success. My mother used to be furious at the number of hours I worked while my children were young, because the only thing she knew was raising kids. Because I worked long hours, I knew that I had to make the best of the time that I did have with my kids. I used to tell my mother that it was quality versus quantity. There were times in my life that I had some regrets about the choices I made, but that's a part of life.

My oldest son is turning thirty. We speak nearly every morning about goals, and how much it means to us to be successful. Recently in one of our morning conversations, he told me that he never realized how much I sacrificed to provide him and his brother with everything they had, including countless memories. I told him that they were actually the ones who made the sacrifice by allowing me the opportunity to work towards my goals with total understanding of the time commitment. We both agreed that we are all better off today from the choices that were made many years ago and my regrets are a thing of the past.

There were people I had close relationships with who judged me because suddenly I had more than them. What they didn't recognize was that there was nothing sudden about it. Because of my relentless will to win, I sacrificed a lot at a young age and as a result success came quicker to me than to others my age. People who want fairness aren't willing to put the work in. Actually, the fact that things weren't fair increased my tenacious side.

Another way to get accelerated results is to treat people the way you wish to be treated. Encourage more and complain less. Complaining brings you down and accomplishes nothing. People who have not been tenacious in reaching their goals and dreams may judge you based on having more than what they do. Separate yourself from those types. Celebrate the success of others, and others will celebrate with you.

Finding your tenacious side also helps during times that you feel like you want to throw in the towel. How many people quit just before hitting it big? Are you one who would decide to shoot the ball in a tie game with only seconds left, or take the chance of losing in overtime? If you find that you are looking for reasons to quit, you've not found your tenacious side. **The average person will quit, the tenacious person will develop a mental toughness and will not accept defeat.** I lost my first run in politics, but rather than giving up, it made me want it even more. When I ran the second time, I won overwhelmingly. While you will never win at everything, it is the lessons that you take with you and the desire to get back on the horse that will yield unlimited potential.

According to an article by psychotherapist Amy Morin, mentally strong people don't waste energy on things they cannot control, they do not give up after a failure, nor do they criticize other people's success ("13 Things Mentally Strong People Don't Do", December 2013, http://www.amymorinlcsw.com).

Implementing these suggestions on a daily basis will ensure it all becomes second nature. I used to have a sign that hung over my desk of a Jacqueline Gomez quote that read, "Success in life comes when you simply refuse to give up, with goals so strong that obstacles, failures and loss only act as motivation."

3
Unlocking Shortcuts

A life without goal setting is destined to be a life of mediocrity. Why sit back and envy what other people have when you're capable of having anything that your heart desires?

Have you ever had a time in your life when you get out of bed each day and you do the same thing that you did the day before, or the week before, or the month before? You set your coffee pot timer to go off at six o'clock, you're in the shower by six fifteen, you get out, you dry off, you're dressed, you have your coffee, and head out the door to a job that seems more like a chore than something that you actually enjoy doing. Can you imagine doing this for the better part of your life, getting towards retirement age and looking back saying, "Why didn't I do something that actually brought me happiness at the end of the day?"

But think now, was there ever a time when you were driving to that job that seemed like a chore that you were daydreaming, "What if I won the lottery? The things that I'd be able to do, the places I could go, the people I'd meet and the sheer excitement of doing something that made me happy?" Well

I'm here to tell you that it doesn't take winning the lottery to make that kind of life for yourself. What it does take is imagining that the sky is the limit and that your destiny and your future is totally in your control. There seriously is no goal that you could set that is too big for you to achieve. Even the office of President of the United States takes goal setting.

If your greatest goal is making sure that you get to work on time each day, then trust me when I tell you, the highest level of goal that you achieve, is simply getting to work on time. Is that a story that you want to share with your grandkids one day?

Nothing big happens without the desire to truly want it bad enough. Any goal, large or small, and taking the steps towards making them happen, builds character and confidence. Life becomes very exciting when you start to reach those goals and without it, it's just plain boring. You should also make sure to celebrate goals as they're reached, because that gives you the momentum to keep setting new ones, bigger and better each time.

Tony Robbins says that setting goals is the first step in turning the invisible to the visible. When we purchased the pest control company, our company records had yet to be put into a computer. The business was being run the old-fashioned way on hand-written work orders and typed out invoices. We knew that we were behind the times and that becoming computerized was first and foremost on the priority list.

Now keep in mind, my husband and I had only been married a few short years. Neither one of us had much of a formal education. I had only taken a couple of computer courses that introduced me to computers, which were fairly new back in those days and neither one of us really knew how to run a company. We set a goal for the date that we wanted to have computers up and running. This date was significant, because in Erie, Pennsylvania, the pest control industry starts the minute the snow is melted, and the sun comes out. We had to be ready, because we knew that having our records organized was going to allow us the opportunity to grow our business that much faster and more expediently.

Of course, you have to expect road blocks along the way. We were overwhelmed when we heard the price tag for computerizing our business and we had few financial resources, since everything that we were generating in the business was actually buying the business for us. We were simply mortified when we had to resort to asking his grandparents for a loan so that we would be able to achieve the goal of having everything done for the start of our season in April.

Our grandparents gave us a three-year term on a $15,000 computer purchase. I was able to get all the information into the computer and run the programs for both our customer records and our accounting by the deadline of the first of April.

Having those records on computer did exactly what I thought it was going to do. It was going to make us more efficient in the way that we were able to run the business. We had such tremendous growth that first year as a result of us being able to run our routes more effectively with the use of the computers. Our cash flow also improved because our billing was now computer generated.

My new goal now was to make sure to pay our grandparents back as quickly as we could, even though their terms were thirty-six months interest-free. The entire $15,000 loan was paid back to them in the first eight months and we never had to ask them for another loan.

When setting goals, you need to put an end date because this gives you a sense of urgency. You have to remember, your day-to-day life is going to get in the way at times. There are many resources available to help you stay on task so that you can achieve these goals in a very reasonable amount of time. With technology today, you literally have the ability to sit and listen to a book while you're working or driving that can help keep you on task and motivated. Your tasks for each day can be added to a smart phone, complete with reminder alarms.

I daydream about how much more successful I would have been had I had those resources available to me when I was twenty-three years old and running my first business. It's said that highly successful people read nearly thirty books a year, and now with programs such as Audible, you can listen to an entire book in a day.

Having great motivators like my all-time favorite Les Brown as well as Zig Ziglar, and Grant Cardone on audio book will certainly help you keep on track. Tools like this can help keep you motivated, but **motivation requires execution**. The day you quit talking about what you want to do and take the action to do it, will be a day you will never regret. Are you clear on what you want as a result of your efforts? Whether it is raising good kids, having unlimited wealth or something as simple as having two consecutive days off a week, you have to have intent before any of this can happen. If you find yourself complaining about what you don't have or what you aren't doing, you will be slowing down or completely stalling your capability of making any of it a reality.

When I was going through treatment for chronic pain I was introduced to a massage therapist through my chiropractor. While having a massage, most people go into a peaceful Zen-like mode. That was never the case for me. The time that I was spending with my massage therapist, Steve Trohoske, was spent talking wildly about ideas that would make us each more money.

Steve reminded me of a younger version of myself, even though we were only a few years apart age-wise. I had the advantage of getting an early start on my career and goals. Steve was not only a very talented massage therapist, he is an amazingly talented jazz bass player. He had focused his younger years on his music as a career. By the time he met his lovely wife, Lena, and started a family, time had ticked by.

We often talked about how he felt like he was spinning his wheels, working as a musician and therapist but not seeing the financial results for the amount of time he was putting in. Lena was working from home as an artist. She specializes in one-of-a-kind jewelry pieces, many made from Steve's broken bass strings as well as paintings and mosaic art. Working on her designs from home allowed her time as a mother to focus on their young children.

Our weekly chat sessions often turned into to talking about the frustrations of working so much, but not getting ahead. The Trohoske's had so much talent between them, but it seemed that others were able to capitalize off their effort as much as they were. For instance, Lena would work tirelessly to create enough art to host an art show at a local gallery. Steve and his bands would often be hired to play at this same gallery.

He and I talked about his and his wife's dreams of what it would be like if they could own their own gallery rather than paying someone for use of theirs. When the Trohoske's started to put their focus on making it happen, rather than simply talking about a dream, doors started opening for them. They found a small space to start a gallery and quickly outgrew it. Today they have one of the community's premiere galleries, where not only is Lena able to create and sell her own art, they are selling consignment art from a variety of local artists as well as hosting art classes for kids. Steve's band still plays for gallery events and the rewards now belong one-hundred percent to them.

Several years ago, it seemed that every day new opportunities were presenting themselves to me. One day at a networking breakfast I had a business associate and friend, Phil Kerner, hand me a DVD and say to me, "This is happening to you right now." I wasn't quite sure what he was talking about, but I tucked the DVD into my bag and it went home with me where it sat next to my TV for a few weeks, until one night I popped it in the DVD player. The DVD was called *The Secret* by Rhonda Byrne, and boy, was Phil right. My life was being played out as if I were an example in the book. *The Secret* talks about the quantum physics behind the laws of the universe, the laws of attraction. There are several professionals and scientists in the book who talk about how your thoughts become reality. When I look back at that period of my life and how things were different, I had a shift in my attitude and my thinking. I was wanting more and more because I was reaching the goals that I was setting and when you do that, your confidence and desires grow to levels I can't even describe.

I was now setting goals in my brain that I didn't even realize that I was putting out there until they came back to me. I'll never forget a conversation that I had with my business partner. It was the day we were included in a press conference with community business leaders that had worked on the ABC hit show *Extreme Makeover*. I told my business partner on the way to the car that I was going to get an account that would be worth twenty-six locations for our pest control company, after an introduction that I had just had with the owner of those locations.

My business partner responded by saying, "You will never get those accounts." That day I literally planted the seed in my brain that those accounts were already ours. A few short months later, I received a call from their regional manager asking for a meeting with me to discuss providing them with a proposal for twenty-six locations. Two months later we were twenty-six locations richer in our pest control business.

Many of the books that I've read on successful people point out that one of the reasons that people are reluctant to set goals is that they're actually afraid of what might happen when they achieve them. It's as if they're somehow not worthy of it, or they're actually afraid of it.

The doors of opportunity started opening for me when I started surrounding myself with people who were setting goals and doing everything to achieve them, knowing that the only limit would be those you personally place on yourself. They were the movers and the shakers of the community and now I was becoming one of them too.

Paving your road to success is so much better when you have people alongside you that are there to inspire, to act as cheerleader, and to offer you every reason why you can do it, not all the reasons why you can't.

There will always come a time when you're going to run into people who are not as motivated as you are. There are many reasons why people like to criticize or try to talk you into believing that something that you've set out to do is simply impossible. Don't allow these people in your life to define you.

Once while speaking in a college entrepreneur class, I had a young man ask me, "What do you do if you have a partner in business who does not believe in setting goals like you do?" Jokingly I answered, "Divorce him." Your goals are for you.

They're not for anybody else, so don't ever worry about what somebody else's opinion of your goal is.

I was now using a combination of techniques that I didn't even realize were coming together to help me achieve my goals. Every chance I got, I was listening to Les Brown on YouTube, talking about how you need to be hungry. I would go to bed at night with the DVD *The Secret* playing, so that I would subliminally have that message replaying over and over in my head as I slept.

And finally, I took the suggestion of *The Secret* and I became a big proponent of vision boarding. One to two times a year for several years now, I cut and paste pictures that are reflective of the upcoming goals that I wish to achieve. I display this board where I'm going to see it several times a day to help remind me to keep my eye on the prize. I could literally write a book on the number of things I manifested: from relationships, to financial windfalls, to the very home I'm living in today.

Once at a vision board party, I was looking desperately for a picture of a boat. I hadn't owned a boat in years and thought it would be nice to have one again. My dear friend, Dr. Stan, had just cut a boat out of a magazine for his own project. He decided that I should have the picture. Literally less than two weeks later I stumbled across a gentleman who was trying to sell his boat. His wife was expecting a child and they needed the money more than the toy. An hour after meeting him, I was writing a check for a custom-designed Pittsburgh Steeler themed boat. I was the envy of the lake that season. At the end of a rainy summer, I decided that I didn't want to go through the work of winterizing it. I posted it for sale online and immediately sold it for more than I had purchased it.

Things like this don't happen by accident, they happen by intent. I'm not suggesting for a second that simply looking at pictures on a vision board will bring you prosperity. What it is designed to do is act as a constant reminder to keep your focus on the positive. On each of my vision boards, I always include the word "grateful".

I have to chuckle today because when my kids were teenagers, they used to make fun of me for some of the things I used to put on my vision boards. That is, until they saw with their own eyes the number of goals that had been achieved through what they saw on my display.

Now my boys are in charge of the business, and they're starting to implement the same techniques that I used through their own goal setting. You can see today how my kids and I have come full circle. I taught them what I learned about success and now that at age fifty-three I'm starting to launch a new career, my boys are instrumental in helping me learn new techniques for promotion. Things that I never imagined having when I was their age and starting out in business – such as Twitter, Instagram and Snapchat.

Recently my oldest son, Ryan, gave me a gift that I use every day. It's the 10X Planner by Grant Cardone that Ryan started using for his own goal setting techniques. I mentioned earlier in the chapter how life is going to cause distractions. Utilizing something such as this planner helps you keep yourself on task day to day, discipline yourself to make sure that you schedule each and every hour of every day with good intentions, and follow through. As a result, even the biggest distraction will not become an obstacle.

In your 10X planner, in addition to planning out each hour of your day, you are also writing down your goals and your target on how to reach those goals in, then documenting your successes each day (remember I pointed out how important it is to celebrate successes, no matter what size they come in). It also has an area for you to list a daily quote. It's recommended that you learn quotes to keep you on track and inspired. Much like the theory behind the vision boarding from *The Secret*, when you look at your goals repetitively, day in and day out, along with how you are going to achieve them, after sixty days the probability of you reaching your goals increases dramatically.

In April of 2017 I started to write the opening chapter to this book. After a series of really bad events, I had quit writing altogether. When Ryan gave me the planner this past February, one of my top goals was to finish and publish this very book. It literally took less than one month of writing the goal down and reading it each and every day until I saw a Facebook advertisement come across my thread several times on how to get your book finished and published.

On April 3rd, which happens to be my youngest son Shane's birthday, I attended a seminar, and as a result you're reading this book. I'm starting to feel again like I did years ago when my friend gave me the copy of *The Secret*. I remember at times people telling me that they thought that I was truly the luckiest person on earth, but I always told them, luck has nothing to do with anything. When you start to take action and align yourself for the success that you desire, you will be absolutely amazed at the opportunities that will present themselves. **You are the creator of your own destination.**

4

Mentors to Millions

*I*f you were going to start a business or buy an existing business and you asked me what my greatest piece of advice would be, I would tell you that first and foremost, I would find a great mentor. Sadly, I was never offered that piece of advice, so it took me nearly fifteen years of trial and error and losing a lot of money trying to figure things out on my own.

It wasn't until I got out from behind my desk and got involved with my community at different networking events that I met some of the most successful people in my community. Many of the dynamic people that I met I had envied for years. Somehow, I was living under this false notion that these people who were so successful must have had it somehow handed to them, and that they achieved their success because they had greater opportunity than I was ever given. I could not have been more wrong.

There are many stories of extraordinary entrepreneurs who started out with little to nothing and accomplished things beyond their wildest dreams. My own mentor, Les Brown, tells the story about he and his twin brother being born in an abandoned warehouse and adopted by Miss Mamie Brown. He shares the struggles that he had growing up being labelled as the "dumb twin" by educators. But like many notable entrepreneurs, he was not going to become a victim of anybody's opinion. While speaking of his accomplishments over the years, he is always quick to share stories of the people who mentored him to greatness.

So how do you find a good mentor? You do what I did, and you look at the people who are where you'd like to be – whether it be in personal or professional lives – and surround yourself with them. I'm sure at one point in your life, you've heard the old adage that success breeds success. Mentors are the people in this world who have not necessarily blazed the trail, but opened their hearts and their minds to learning from those who had used mentors themselves. The great Bob Proctor characterizes a mentor as "someone who sees more talent and ability within you, than you see in yourself, and helps bring it out of you."

When considering a good mentor you should look outside your inner circle. It's not often wise to choose a friend or a family member, because you may not get the clarity or the honesty that you would from somebody who is not afraid to tell you the truth.

You need someone who won't put their personal feelings above the facts.

In an article by Sheila Eugenio ("7 Reasons You Need a Mentor For Entrepreneurial Success", http://entrepreneur.com, August 17, 2016) she states that nearly 70% of the businesses that survived the first five years attributed it to the fact that they had a mentor who helped get them over the hurdles in the early stages. Would you rather be learning through trial and error, and spending and wasting a lot of your own money in doing so? Or does it make greater sense to learn from those who have already done it?

A good mentor is going to push you to learn. They're not going to offer you all the answers, but a good mentor will help you learn from the mistakes they made. You need to trust and listen to their experiences. I only wish that somebody had given me this piece of advice when I was twenty-three years old and new to business.

Why do you think that the greatest athletes on earth have coaches? It's because no matter how talented you may be at something, you'll always need that second set of eyes looking at you, who is able to tell you things about you that you don't see in yourself. But you do have to be open-minded enough to welcome it as something other than criticism. If you're a person who tends to take things personally, then I'm going to tell you right now that if you want to excel, get over it.

Having a strong, trusted mentor gives you the capability of becoming the best version of yourself. In 2006 at a networking event, I was asked by Linda Stevenson if I would apply for the Athena Powerlink mentoring program that is offered to women who own businesses. At that point I looked back and recall being a little bit arrogant, thinking, why do I need mentoring? I've already been running my own business for fifteen years. I started the application and eventually it ended up in the trash, because I thought I had better things to do with my time.

Fast forward two years later, after I was involved in many community events, networking organizations, and meeting the most dynamic people in business. I was approached again by Linda Stevenson about the Athena program. Linda had already identified that I'd be a good candidate because I was running a well-known family business, but also saw that I had a lot of room for growth. I'm thankful to this day that she gave me a second chance at the offer to apply. The more time I was spending with successful people, the more I realized I still had a lot I needed to learn. The Athena Powerlink application included the submission of my business plan. I had never even read a business plan, let alone written one for my business. I was amazed at how much I learned just putting together that business plan for the application. You can imagine how excited and amazed I was when I received the phone call from Linda that I was selected as a finalist. The thought of having my business put under a magnifying glass by some of my city's top professionals was a little nerve-wracking at first. But then I realized that people pay $40,000 to $60,000 for these kinds of consulting services, and I would be receiving them free of charge if chosen. It just made total sense.

During my interview, I was actually asked by the panel if I was coachable. When being mentored, you need to have an open mind. You need to be open to criticism and you need to realize that the way you do things may not be the most efficient way. After a year of having every angle of the business reviewed, I started to implement the suggestions made by my mentors. I received the most valuable advice from attorneys, CPAs and even marketing people from General Electric Company. It was amazing the things I was learning about a business that I had been running for fifteen years.

I went into the mentoring program with the impression that our greatest profits were being made on our commercial accounts, only to find out that I was putting my focus at the wrong end of our business. This is why I wasn't seeing the growth that I had seen when I first took over. After taking on the advice and changing the direction of how and who I was selling to, our company realized a 25% increase in the first full year following my Athena Powerlink mentoring.

I was blessed to be part of such a valuable program. While the Athena Powerlink program is unique to women in businesses, there are professional mentoring services available free of charge to people who either want to start a business, or are at a plateau and need a business professional to take a look from the outside.

Doors of opportunity were opening for me regularly now. Shortly after finishing my mentoring program, I was asked to become a mentor with the SCORE Program, which is the nation's largest network of volunteer expert business mentors. SCORE is a partner to the United States Small Business Administration that has helped over 11 million entrepreneurs. It was such an honor for me to be asked to participate as a counsellor for SCORE. Alongside top executives from a variety of different industries, I was more than grateful to be able to give my time to others as those had given time to me.

Just two short years prior, I had never read nor written a business plan, and now I was in a position to actually assist others in doing exactly that, as a foundation for their business idea. Unknowingly, I had become a mentor to people in my community who acted on what I suggested, and started spending time with me to see how I was able to be at the top of my game.

Once I had a young lady, Tiffani Staley, attend an event I was hosting. Afterward she asked if I would be willing to spend some time with her to discuss a business idea that she had. Tiffani came to my office for a meeting. I learned that she sought me out after seeing me in the local news for something business, community, or politically related. She told me that she knew the importance of surrounding herself with the people who are "doing", not just talking about it. I was so honored to know that I had caught the attention of a young entrepreneur who was anxious to learn from me. It was my chance to pay it forward. Later, Tiffani and I lost touch for a short time. I will never forget the day that I opened an email from her telling me that she had completed business school at the top of her class, and that she would be honored if I would attend her graduation. That honor was all mine! It is years later, and to this day I consider her one of my dearest friends.

Earlier I talked about how you shouldn't choose people in your inner circle, because you want somebody who is going to give you the hard truth whether you want to hear it or not. It is difficult as a mentor to tell somebody that the idea that they're bringing to the table may not be something that will pan out in the long run. **As a mentor, you never want to set somebody up for failure, but it's also not your job to be the final decision maker.** A good mentor is going to point out the pros and cons and offer advice on how things might have been done in their own business. But again, ultimately the decision is that of the entrepreneur. I listened to and trusted the people who were helping me recreate myself and the way I was running my business and the results were phenomenal. I have also seen the flipside where people didn't take the advice of their mentor, and as a result not only lost their business but lost their life savings.

One of my favorite shows to watch is *Shark Tank*. This is where aspiring entrepreneurs bring their ideas to people who are already highly successful. On the show they have the opportunity of partnering not only to benefit from their expert advice, but also as investors. It always amazes me when one of the "sharks" shows interest in investing in a business, yet the entrepreneur challenges the knowledge and suggestions the experts are making. Understand, these people didn't become multi-millionaires and billionaires by accident. Most of these "sharks" came from humble backgrounds, just like the people who are pitching their ideas to them on the show. There's no doubt in my mind that these experts took the advice of their mentors when they were launching their own businesses.

I will ask you just as I was asked in my interview, **are you coachable?** When enlisting the help of other mentors, aim high. Let them know how serious and dedicated you are in making your dream become a reality. Showing your passion will not only help to encourage you to reach your goals, it will show those who are mentoring you that you are worth every ounce of their time and energy to help you achieve the same success that they've achieved in their own lives. I was truly blessed having my Athena Powerlink mentors. Linda once joked that the program is estimated to be worth nearly $40,000 in consulting, "but for Donna Rae, it was worth $80,000 because she was relentless in her quest for their help and time."

Do you think that you can reach your goals and dreams faster through trial and error? Or would you be making a better business decision by enlisting the help of those who have already done it?

Keep in mind also that the business climate is constantly changing. There's no such thing as being too old or too experienced to continually enlist the help of others. Two months ago I turned fifty-three. When I made the conscious decision to start working towards a new career I knew I needed the support of others. Not only was I working to resolve chronic health issues that took tremendous focus, I was living in a different state and had zero connections.

This wasn't something I was familiar with. In my hometown, I got to know everyone from being involved in business, community and local politics. Thankfully when I stumbled across Les Brown's program, it opened many doors of opportunity to meet amazing new mentors. I may be a seasoned entrepreneur and business person, but there's still a lot I need to learn if I want to be successful in an entirely new career.

While I know a lot about how to start a company from years of experience and the coaching that I once offered, in order to obtain maximum results, I had no problem investing in new learning by hiring some of the country's top coaches and mentors. I had the choice of taking the time to figure it out on my own, but I'm in the over-fifty crowd now and would rather be on the fast track with help from those who are already there.

Now I am working with world-renowned speakers, authors and entrepreneurs that are more successful than I ever imagined that I could be, until now. And with the use of technology, I am able to meet daily with my mentors, face-to-face, from whatever part of the globe they happen to be in. The more information that they provide to me, the more and more I want. I would be lying if I told you that working with millionaires like Les Brown, Omar Periu and Antonio T. Smith Jr. wasn't a bit intimidating at first. Later I realized that I am just like them, each of us from humble beginnings, and that our desire for success makes us all unstoppable. The only thing that sets us apart at the end of the day, is the amount of money that goes into our vault earned through our efforts.

Remember the difference between advice and opinion when you are seeking any kind of growth through a mentor or coach. Advice is something that is given based on learning through experience. Opinions are not facts, they are judgements and beliefs that may or may not be true. Having a flashy business card or website does not qualify a person as a mentor or coach. Having real life experience and the success to show for it are the key components when looking to enlist this kind of help. A good mentor or coach is someone who can share with you their success by showing it to you, not just give examples of what it could look like. Multi-millionaire best-selling author and entrepreneurial coach, Omar Periu not only shares pictures of his estates, he invites you to his home for his mastermind sessions. Would you rather learn from the advice of someone who has lived it, or the opinion of someone who simply wants to invoice you at the end of the day?

My favorite tweegram reads, "It's so essential to surround yourself with individuals who are already where you want to be. Iron sharpens iron."

5
Sell It!

*W*hy not have the life that you deserve? The best is out there for all of us, so now how do you go and get it? The answer is sales.

Selling is literally connected to everything that we do. I'm not just talking about money being exchanged for goods and services after a sale. We're selling ourselves on relationships all the time without even realizing it. There is literally no limit on what you're able to sell.

In the words of Jim Rohn, "Become a millionaire, not for the million dollars, but for what it will make of you to achieve it" (*Leading an Inspiring Life*, Nightingale-Conant, 1996). If you're trying to sell something that doesn't interest you, how could you expect the person that you're targeting to be interested?

If you do not completely believe in what you are selling, you either need to figure out your reluctance before attempting to sell it, or you are destined to fail. You must be able to sell yourself on your product before being able to effectively sell it to anyone else. It would be like a car salesman attempting to convince you that the Ford is the best choice, yet driving a

Chevy himself. Consider a sales call an audition. In order to land the lead role, you must be better than those competing against you.

In my early years after buying the pest control company, I didn't get involved because it was something that excited me: I got into it because my husband at the time needed my help. I quickly learned that in order to grow the business, I had to believe in what I was selling when a client contacted me.

My interest wasn't in the biology of insects; I had a passion for problem solving. And anyone who was calling our business needed a problem solved. My selling tactic turned into showing the potential new client that I had compassion for what they were going through and that added value in what we were offering versus what they were getting from our competition, who simply offered a price.

I needed to be passionate about what I was offering, or the company would fail.

We were too small and had limited financial resources to hire a salesperson, so the sale needed to be made when the client called the first time, or we would lose them to our competition, a chain operator who had professional salespeople.

Selling can't end at five o'clock when your workday ends if you want to reach and exceed your goals. I never missed a chance at getting in on a conversation if overhearing people talk about an insect problem that they were dealing with. For example, one summer when I had my dog in obedience school, one of the pet owners was asking the trainer the best way to avoid a flea problem.

I simply started sharing my knowledge of this problem, not mentioning that I owned a pest control company until the pet owner asked me how I was so knowledgeable. I didn't approach the subject as if I was trying to sell my service, but rather offering information from one pet owner to another.

A good salesperson is able to attract a buying audience by having the ability to sell themselves first. The pet owner never knew that my intent was to sell her our goods and services, but that's exactly what happened.

Entrepreneurs never set limits, nor make excuses when it comes to selling. A successful entrepreneur would take a commission job over a salaried job on any given day. Commissions come with unlimited earning potential, where salaried positions tend to encourage mediocrity because there are no rewards in going above and beyond.

One of the biggest reasons that people don't succeed in sales is their lack of commitment to it. Recently I was listening to Gary Vaynerchuk who shares his business model in public speaking engagements all over the world. Gary had somebody in the audience ask him why he shares all his strategies that have helped him earn millions. He responded that due to people's lack of commitment, less than 1% of those in attendance would actually ever follow through in copying his strategy, therefore they were not a threat to him.

Many people work with great ambition, but ambition and commitment are two different things. An ambitious person will go to work and give it their all during their eight-hour work day. An ambitious person is going to set a quota for the day and once it's reached they become complacent and satisfied with the minimum. A committed person is already going to have goals set before even arriving at their place of employment. A committed person is going to stay on task throughout their work day and continue to sell beyond their work day looking for any opportunity that may present itself.

Success-driven entrepreneurs have a win-at-all-cost attitude. These ego-driven people enjoy being competitive. Take a track athlete for instance. The best athletes measure their success in breaking their own records each time they compete, continually striving for their personal best. Having this determination, they work tirelessly through practice and preparation. The best athletes have fully committed themselves to being winners.

The same should apply to anything that you're selling.

Another key component to being the best salesperson you can be is **active listening**. You may know your products and services inside and out, as well as the value that it will bring to a person. But I don't know anyone who likes a hard sell. The hard sell salesperson is the "in your face, you need me and I'm going to tell you why" type of person.

Once I had a radio advertising salesperson come to my place of business without any appointment. I happened to be in the middle of working on a proposal for one of my own clients with a deadline that was just around the corner. I offered this woman the opportunity to make an appointment to sit down and go over what she wanted to talk about at a later date. She immediately went into her sales pitch, telling me about my need for her service and that I should just take the time now to listen to the sample recording that the radio station had made, it would only take five minutes of my time.

I very professionally asked her once again if she would like to make an appointment for a future date. She continued on her canned sales pitch. It was then that I turned to the other people in my office and I asked if I was not being articulate enough. The saleswoman abruptly picked up the sample DVD and told me that it was my loss that I didn't take the time to listen to her.

Not only would I never buy a product from that station, I called the owner of the station and told them that under no circumstances do I ever want a salesperson from their company coming to my business again. Whether the product that she had to offer was good or not, she chose not to listen when I told her that my need was to sit down with her at a later date.

Active listening also requires you to be present when you are selling to a person. I've seen dramatic changes over my twenty-five years as an entrepreneur. While smart phones make things more efficient, they also act as a major distraction when it comes to being present in the moment. Once at our monthly networking meeting, I decided to demonstrate to seventy-five entrepreneurs how their smart phone may be hampering their own growth in sales. I instructed each of the entrepreneurs to place their phone in the basket that was in the middle of the table so that for the hour they were spending with other entrepreneurs exchanging ideas, they could have total focus. Nearly fifty percent of these business professionals, who were taking time out of their day for a networking event to help grow their sales and businesses, spent more time focusing on their smart phone.

On more than one occasion I have had a salesperson in my business trying to sell me something, and the minute they referred to their phone for an email or text, I would promptly end the appointment with them. Not being present in the moment tells your potential new client that your time is more valuable than theirs.

I once wrote an article for a small business magazine titled, "Smart phones, dumb people." I went on to explain that having the ability to read a text or an email the moment it's received is not always productive. As a matter of fact, in sales, it can be counterproductive. Being able to multi-task is one thing, but shifting your attention from your client to your phone demonstrates a lack of professionalism. Before this technology, it was acceptable to address an email when you were done with a client, but now it seems that the expectations of both the sender and the receiver require immediate attention. Call me "old school", but if I'm being asked to spend money with someone, requiring their undivided attention should not be too much to ask.

I was never a fan of cold calling myself, because I didn't appreciate when people would show up and disrupt my workday without an appointment. However, cold calling is a necessity. When cold calling, I was always prepared with business cards and brochures that I could leave with a potential new client, even if I was only stopping by their place of business to ask for an appointment on a later date to sit down and discuss their needs.

When I ran for political office I wasn't looking for financial gain, but I was looking for votes. Again, I was selling myself. I knocked on countless doors, handing out my brochures, but never expecting to impinge on people's time. If they wanted to talk to me, then I was happy to spend as much time as they needed.

Most of the people that you're going to be selling to have some kind of assistant who will be your first point of contact. I like to refer to that person as the gatekeeper. Keep in mind that the gatekeeper likely encounters many people a week trying to sell something to their employer. How you act and treat the gatekeeper on the initial contact can play a significant role in how soon that message will be delivered. The people who acted as my gatekeepers knew the types of salespeople that I was not interested in talking to.

Always treat the gatekeeper with respect and courtesy.

Some of the tips that I've learned from over twenty-five years of experience reading books and listening to some of the greatest salespeople on earth are:

1. Be assertive not aggressive. Aggressive is demanding a decision immediately, while the assertive approach would be to ask, "What is the best time to follow up with you?"
2. Allow the buyer to learn more about you by the questions you ask them.
3. If you're met with reluctance to what you're selling, try to get to the bottom of why the buyer is uncomfortable.
4. Be empathetic, but don't ever try to solve a problem until you fully understand what their situation really is.
5. Treat the person who is reluctant to buy from you with the same respect as the person who jumps at the opportunity to buy from you.

There are many variables as to why people may not impulse buy, but I can assure you that if you work on building a relationship, when they are ready you will be the first person that comes to mind. This very thing just happened to me.

While at the Les Brown retreat I attended a breakout session with Antonio Smith, Jr. I was intrigued, because the presentation was about accelerating your earning potential. After only five minutes of talking about himself and his company, he went right to the audience to ask if there were any questions that he could answer relevant to the subject matter. Of course, I was quick to raise my hand to ask questions, because at fifty-three years old, I'm coming out of retirement and starting a whole new career. After forty-five minutes of listening to the most incredible sales information, I had to leave for another commitment. Once I returned home from the retreat and I was going through my notes, I came across Antonio's page. I reached out to him via Facebook Messenger and he immediately returned my call. I apologized for having to leave his presentation early and I asked if he could tell me what I had missed. I was hoping that his presentation was ultimately going to be something that he was selling, because I wanted it.

As it turns out, he was offering his sales program at a deeply discounted rate for those who were in attendance that day. Several weeks after working with Antonio, his staff and his clients, I shared the secret that I would have paid full price, because I was overwhelmingly impressed with the knowledge of what he was selling.

Once I suggested to a massage therapist that she should be giving free mini chair massages at our networking events. She replied, "I don't give my service away for free." Don't ever be afraid to discount or provide your service for free initially to obtain a new client. If you believe in your product enough to know that they are going to return for more, then consider the discount or free rate as marketing and advertising expense.

Do you think the massage therapist would gain more clients from a $1,000 coupon campaign by mail, or by providing a sample of her service? Five minutes could have easily turned into a new client willing to pay $60 per hour for her service. Instead, she looked at it as losing money by giving something away for free. She would have had to provide 16.66 hours of free service just to break even on the $1,000 ad campaign. She clearly did not understand the importance of selling herself.

People today can buy just about any product online for less than what you may be selling it for. It is imperative that you are sold on your product in order to convince a person that even if they are spending a bit more, your company, product, or customer service is worth the extra money that they are spending with you.

Our pest control company offers "do it yourself" products. We understand that not everyone has the financial resources to hire professional services, and some are simply more comfortable doing their own work. Being a small company, we don't have the volume buying power that the big box stores have when it comes to retail products.

There were times when I would see products in chain retail stores for sale to the public for less than what we were able to buy wholesale. I had to provide more value than simply selling a product if I expected people to spend more with me. Since I had a strong belief in the added value, I didn't have to spend much time convincing people that the extra money they were spending was worth it.

The value that we added was our knowledge. Customers would often bring insects in to our office to have them identified. Once identified, we would take the time to walk them through how to use the "do it yourself" products to solve their problem, allowing them to ask as many questions as they needed until they felt comfortable enough to use a chemical in their own home. They were buying more than a product, they were buying our years of expertise.

Of course we would have the occasional customer call to complain that they saw a product at a big box store for less and that we somehow ripped them off. I was always quick to ask if the cashier at the checkout line was able to identify their problem and instruct them on the solution with the product they were buying. For some, price is all that matters. For those types, you could be the best salesperson on the planet and still not get the sale.

How do you like to be treated as a customer? Would you rather be served with respect and a smile, or from someone acting as if they are doing you a favor? To be the best sales person possible, live by the Golden Rule: "do unto others as you would have them do unto you." People will pay any amount for something they love. It's your job to make them love you!

6
Fail to Win

*F*ailures are temporary.

The greatest successes can come from learning from your past mistakes. How will you possibly ever know success if you don't take the risk? Even if that means failing at the first attempt, learn from it. Failure should never be your defining moment, it should only act as a tool for how to do it differently the next time around.

Henry Ford once said, "Failure is simply the opportunity to begin again, this time more intelligently." Some of the greatest inspirational stories are about people who failed multiple times before finding success. Milton Hershey, for example, had three different failed candy companies before he founded the Lancaster Caramel Company, which would eventually evolve into the Hershey Company, which now has a net worth of over ten billion dollars.

Colonel Sanders is another great example. His recipe was rejected over a thousand times before he ended up starting Kentucky Fried Chicken at fifty-six years of age. Steven Spielberg, worth over three billion dollars, was rejected multiple times by the University of Southern California for Cinematic Arts. A local TV station fired a news reporter; that news reporter would eventually become the queen of daytime talk. That's right – they fired Oprah Winfrey – now with a net worth of over 2.9 billion dollars.

Failures create an emotional experience but failing doesn't have to be fatal. One of my favorite quotes is by Zig Ziglar. He said, "Remember that failure is an event, not a person." I was once given the analogy that it's like a good gym workout. When you first start working out, your muscles are sore and tender, but eventually your muscles will heal and you're going to come out stronger than when you started.

Did you know that Michael Jordan was once cut from his high school basketball team? He was quoted years later in the *Chicago Tribune* saying, "It was good because it made me know what disappointment felt like, and I knew that I didn't want to ever have that feeling ever again" ("When Jordan Cried Behind Closed Doors", May 15, 1991).

Recently I was having a conversation with a gentleman who is not a fan of Donald Trump. He very angrily told me that he heard that Donald Trump had bankrupted more than one business. I explained to him that that was not a rumor, that was an actual fact and that Donald Trump is not the first nor the last billionaire who is going to have failures. I've had failures in both my personal and professional life. But I'd rather have failures than regret. I'd much rather tell my grandkids one day about the chances that I took that may not have worked out, and the lessons that I learned from them, rather than telling them what I wished I had done with my life but hadn't.

At my physical therapy office there's a sign that says, "Don't worry about failures, worry about the chances you miss when you don't even try."

Thomas Edison can be credited with providing us with light bulbs. Did you know that it took him over a thousand times before he was able to perfect it? A reporter once asked Thomas Edison how it felt to fail 1,000 times. He responded by saying, "I didn't fail a thousand times, the light bulb was an invention with a thousand steps."

Choosing to go through life playing it safe tends to give you a life of mediocrity. Most people don't start things with the intention of them not working out. Forty-one percent of first marriages fail. I've never met a married couple in my lifetime who walked down the aisle on their wedding day in anticipation of a divorce in their future. When my husband Jim and I realized that it was becoming increasingly difficult to work together and manage our home together, I actually told him that my greatest fear in divorcing was that I would feel as if I failed.

When I was finally able to look at the optimistic side of being divorced, I realized that I had the opportunity to look back on my role in that failed relationship. I could learn from the mistakes that I made, which in turn would help to make stronger relationships in the future.

It's apparent that not everybody follows the rule of learning from mistakes, because statistics say that second marriages fail at a rate of 60% and third marriages fail at an even greater rate.

I've known entrepreneurs on both sides of the coin. One gentleman I knew very well was great in the restaurant business. In fact, he had multiple successful restaurants throughout his career. His problem was he knew food and he knew how to market his businesses. He was never lacking a good client base. His failure came in the form of money management. A well-known fact is that you need to pay your taxes first; something that he didn't do that got him into trouble more than once. After the third failed restaurant, it was evident he had not changed the means by which he was running his business that got him into trouble the first two times. He eventually ran out of funds as well as resources to help him fund any future projects. Winners analyze, losers rationalize. This goes hand in hand with that old saying, the definition of insanity is doing things the same way over and over again and expecting different results.

Several years ago, I was asked to join a committee for a well-established nonprofit event that was held annually. I was new to the group, so I did more observing and gave input only when asked. After my first year volunteering on the committee, I was asked if I would chair the following year. A lot of hard work went into an event that yielded low returns for the effort that was put forth. At the conclusion of the first year of my chair, the organization was happy with the return, however I wasn't. I was asked if I would chair the following year. I told them that the only way I would agree to do that is that if they allowed me to change the way things were being done in years prior. As a spectator, I was able to see that the focus was on the gross amount of money that was being raised and not the net amount after the expense of hosting it.

The representative that I was working with from the nonprofit was highly reluctant when I told him that I would agree to chair only if I could make changes. It's not that I thought that the nonprofit was failing, but I was confident that their goal of increasing the annual contributions through this event could be achieved through reducing the overheads of hosting the event.

Did I know for certain that the changes that I was going to propose would yield them a greater outcome? No. But after nine years of doing things the same way and not seeing a monetary increase from the amount of time that people invested, I certainly realized that it was worth the attempt. The nonprofit agreed to allow me to make the changes that I thought were necessary to give them a better financial outcome.

My mindset going into that upcoming year was that failure was not an option. We were able to dramatically reduce the expense of hosting the event and thankfully our community embraced the changes that were made and the net return to the nonprofit was thousands more than where I had set the bar.

Another reason why people fail is from having a fatalistic attitude. These are people that contribute both the wins and losses to luck. There is no such thing as luck. I once counselled a person who wanted to start his own business from scratch. He was so excited about his idea that he wasn't open-minded about the "what ifs" that I presented to him.

The role of an entrepreneurial coach is not to tell somebody that he should or shouldn't do something, but rather point out the pros and cons and let him decide for himself. Sometimes I was brutally honest, because in good conscience I don't want to set anyone up for failure. In this particular case I offered a red flag of caution: I pointed out that he had a tremendous amount of franchise competition and also that the space he was looking at running was not only overpriced, but was very inconvenient. This person chose to move forward with his plan, leveraging his retirement savings and his house. I wasn't happy nor surprised to learn that the business had folded and that he was attributing it to bad luck.

I had two different office assistants who left me to buy their own businesses. Much like me, they bought businesses yet had no formal education or experience in running a business.

Both worked side by side with me for a number of years. One assistant kept it quiet until the transaction was complete. The second assistant actually enlisted my help and often asked for advice. She was investing in a small beer distributor that she and her husband would run. At first, I thought it wasn't a bad idea because it was located between two colleges. They had a strong target market. It was announced in our state that legislation would likely pass that would allow beer to be sold in grocery stores. I immediately recommended that she back out of the sale because she would never be able to compete with the wholesale pricing that chain stores had in bulk-buying power. She opted to go through with the purchase anyway. It played out just as I had expected. Years following we ran into each other. She told me that she wished she had taken the advice I had offered. She also said, "You make running a business look easy." Neither business purchased by my assistants would succeed. The question is, were lessons learned in the process?

Years after purchasing the family pest control company, my husband and I stumbled across a cookie gift shop that was for sale. It was winter, and our seasonal business was very quiet. I will admit, buying it was the worst decision ever. We bought it because we were bored. Rather than taking the downtime in the winter to strategize on growing the business we already had, we took on a second that was entirely different from what we were used to. Now we were busy, hands-on, and year round.

We were able to build a small shop for our cookie company on the same property where our pest control company was located. This allowed me the opportunity to be available to both businesses. I found myself running back and forth, from crisis to crisis. Both businesses required a lot of supervision and hand holding. When we first purchased the cookie gift shop, I moved my full-time office into that building so I could focus on growing their sales. As a result, I was watching the numbers in our primary business go backwards. The pest control company was our bread and butter, while the cookie gift shop started out as a winter pastime for entrepreneurs who were bored. I could not allow nor afford losing the growth that we worked so hard to build, and I eventually moved my office back to the pest control building. It took the fear of failure to help me realize my priority. The cookie gift shop would ultimately be sold with many lessons learned.

Part of overcoming mistakes and failures is the ability to look at a situation and own it. Too often it is human nature to simply blame others.

My business partner and I often butted heads when problems in our business would arise. He would focus on trying to convince me that it wasn't his fault. My focus was never on whose fault it was, but rather learning from it, so that the same mistake was not made twice. I remember telling my staff and my partner that the first time is a mistake, the second time is a habit.

How often do you see politicians today who lose a race against their opponent and blame everybody but themselves? Abraham Lincoln lost eight political races through the course of his political career. He didn't quit, because he was committed to serving his country. Those losses no doubt made him a stronger person, which would also help him become a better leader.

I failed in my own first attempt at running for political office. In 2011, I ran for Township Supervisor against an 18-year incumbent. It wasn't that I needed a career change; I was becoming increasingly frustrated with the way my tax dollars were being wasted. With encouragement from my family and the commitment to step up in our family business, I ran. I didn't know the first thing about politics, but I did know how to manage money effectively, something I didn't believe our current leaders were doing. It was early in the primary that I got my feet wet with the reality of politics. The word "dirty" comes to mind. I breezed through the primary race against a guy who would not only be my opponent again, but also my nemesis.

I lost the general election to the incumbent. It would prove to be a failure, but one that I learned a lot from.

Years later, our school district was going through turmoil. I didn't let the loss from the first attempt at public service dampen my involvement in community politics. I started to vocally challenge our school leadership and board. When election time came, I stepped up again.

Gandhi is believed to have said, "Be the change you want to see in the world." I had learned a lot from my first loss and did not allow history to repeat itself. I won this race overwhelmingly. Our district was starting over with a new administration with new people serving on the board. Because we learned from the failures of others, we were able to improve both the education and finances of our district dramatically.

Can you imagine what life would be without the luxury of automobile and airline travel? Had Henry Ford and the Wright Brothers given in to several failed attempts, we may not be as advanced in travel today as a result. It seems incredible that Walt Disney was fired from his job with the Kansas City Star because his editor said that he lacked imagination and had no good ideas. He went on to found Laugh-o-gram Studios, which would go bankrupt, but would continually go back to the drawing board, literally. According to Today.com, Disney World employs over 62,000 people, making it the largest single-site employer in the country.

The most successful people understand that failure is part of the process.

Many entrepreneurs embrace the pain of failure. They have identified that plateaus are part of life. Everyone goes through periods of becoming complacent at times. I remember getting notice that we had lost our single biggest pest control client. It wasn't because we were doing a bad job, it's likely because we had become too comfortable and our competition was able to win over the client by pointing out our weaknesses. Having no forewarning of this loss, I was not able to financially prepare for it. All of a sudden we had to make difficult decisions that included my partner and me taking a deep pay cut, as well as having to lay off our own son because he was the newest full-time employee in the company.

Ordinary people may not survive this kind of hit. Extraordinary people look at it and capitalize on it.

My son who was now out of work and barely surviving on unemployment started delving into the reasons that we may have lost this account. How was our competition able to identify our weaknesses? By figuring this out, when the contract was up for renewal he was ready to go back after it with even greater confidence. His future with the family business was contingent upon the success he would have in getting this client back. He knew that we were better equipped to handle the demands, but we had done it for so long that we may have taken it for granted. Not only did he learn from the mistakes we made as a company, he capitalized on our competition's weaknesses and was able to secure the client for more money than we were charging before losing them.

I recently heard an analogy about a baby that was learning how to walk. They fall over and over again, yet continue to get back up and try all over again. Everybody is aware that babies are eventually going to walk, so each of their falls are met with encouragement to get up and try it again. There's nobody there discouraging them from learning. The next time you fall, remember that the ability to get up and walk again that you were born with.

Of all the quotes that I share from Les Brown, one of my favorites is, "When you fall down, try to land on your back. Because if you're looking up, you can get up."

7
Niche

very single one of us has unique DNA that makes us stand out.

Having a "niche" is getting to the root of who you are, the product that you're offering, and the ability to be in full alignment with what you put into the market. Your niche needs to be specific and easily understandable to your ideal client.

You have to have confidence in your niche. Be genuine, otherwise people will be turned off. It is impossible to be the best at everything, so finding your niche is key.

Knowing your niche makes it easier to explain to potential clients what it is that you do or sell by being very specific. If you are in the process of making the decision to start your own business, do the research before choosing which business.

I shared a post on Facebook that said 99% of failures come from people who have a habit of making excuses. I was immediately challenged by a friend who pointed out the high percentage of businesses that fail in the first five years. He gave the example of the number of restaurants that go out of business quickly, in spite of investing a lot of hard work, money and time. He said that as an entrepreneur myself, I should know how difficult it is to run a successful business. I assured him that it isn't easy and if it was, then everybody would be doing it.

But reflecting back to the original post, I let him know that I owned my mistakes and learned from them. Then I asked him why he thought that a large percentage of restaurants go out of business in the first five years. Could it be that the market is saturated and that the research before opening a restaurant was insufficient? If you opened a new business that was unique, or had something that set it apart from the competition, would the success rate be more favorable?

When my grandfather-in-law started our pest control company in 1932, there were literally two companies in the phone book to choose from. By the time we purchased it three generations later, there were six pages in the phone book, front and back, with a combination of both family-owned and chain pest control companies to choose from. In the days of having to resort to a phone book to hire any business, it was more about who had the biggest ad than a specific reputation. Since we were a small family-owned business, there was no way we would ever have the advertising dollars to compete with national chains. We had to find our niche so that the advertising dollars that we did have were reaching the right audience.

When people called our office looking for help the first time, I started polling people. I knew that by the time they called our business, it was likely that they had called every big ad in the book looking for the best price. What I learned through polling my customers was that the competition was insistent on sending a salesperson to their home to look at the problem before they would discuss the price with them. When dealing with a pest control issue, most people don't want to wait for someone to solve their problem, they want it done now. I found our niche.

I understood why the competition wanted to send a salesperson out, because people are more likely to buy face-to-face in most cases. Our competition was also using the face-to-face sales tactic to add on what I consider to be unnecessary annual contracts. I say unnecessary, because pest control in the north is a six month out of a 12-month business for residential clients. I didn't feel right selling services for six months out of the year that I knew people would not need.

What also set us apart from our competition was the fact that when you called our business, you were actually talking to somebody who would be able to help you with your immediate need. When calling the chain companies, often you would be in contact with a call center that may not even be located in the United States. When calling our local competition, most times it was an answering service and you would have to wait for a return call.

We certainly had a niche.

First, whoever answered the phone had to know how to identify and solve the problem without having to send anyone to look at it. Second, we could give a price for that service in that initial phone call. Third, because we had done the sale on the phone, we were able to schedule the work to be done before our competition either returned the phone call or sent a salesman out to look at a problem.

We took those three key components and used them for our target advertising during our seasonal months.

There actually was a time, long before the use of smart phones, that all we had in the phone book was a listing with our name on it. With our niche, we were no longer wasting advertising dollars on phone book ads that nobody even read six months out of the year. Rather than trying to be more like our competition, we did exactly the opposite of what they were doing to obtain new clients. Then we were backing these sales up with integrity by not selling services and contracts that our client didn't need. I never offered a cost for the solution until I had explained what their problem was and how we were going to solve it. We quickly learned that people who were simply looking for the bottom line price were not the target market that we were looking for.

We're now in our fourth generation and still growing. There's nothing more rewarding than when a client thanks you for your honesty and integrity, and when they realize that we were more concerned about their results than charging for services they didn't need.

I've explained more than once that we've been in business for over eighty years, and that doesn't happen by accident. If you've been in business and you're not seeing the results that you were hoping for, maybe it is because you haven't found your niche. If you're not sure what it is, don't be afraid to enlist the help of others who are familiar with your business. Ask them what they think it is that sets you apart from your competition. If that doesn't work, don't be afraid to hire somebody externally who can look at your business with an objective eye. **Sometimes a niche requires disrupting what's normal.**

My son's girlfriends, Alexis and Kelli, have been brainstorming about opening their own business together. Each one of them has different qualities and experience that they can bring to the table. The idea that they have been tossing around is a great one, but they realize that the industry might be a bit saturated in their area. This is where coming up with a unique idea that is going to set them apart from their competition is crucial before simply opening the doors. Through their brainstorming sessions, they came up with an idea that would make them completely unique in the entire city.

The next hurdle is, how do you get the message out when you have limited marketing dollars? I suggested to them that they needed to come up with a name that people were not going to forget. Something that would disrupt the normal. A name that people would not only not forget about but would be so intriguing that they would talk about it. They are taking the time to research who their target market will be, including the ages, the demographics and the income levels of their potential buyers. I will predict that the day that these girls put their plan in motion, they will not be one of the statistics of businesses that close in the first five years.

One of my favorite examples of someone who disrupts the normal is a funeral director friend of mine. I actually met him years ago at one of the many networking events where we seemed to keep bumping into each other. Face it, the career of a funeral director would have to be somewhat of a depressing one. That kind of a business also relies heavily on building relationships, because when a loved one passes, you want to work with people you know, like and trust. I became a big fan of Jack Martin, because he found his niche by taking a very heavy subject and making it comfortable to talk about. During the thirty second commercial portion of the event, his focus was on the importance of preplanning your funeral to help take that burden away from your family. At our networking breakfast, Jack would end his thirty second elevator pitch with the tag line, "We put the fun in funerals."

I knew that when the time came, this was someone that I could do business with. Sadly, that time did come, when my brother was diagnosed with terminal cancer. I made the suggestion that they meet with my new friend Jack Martin to discuss their needs. Because Jack took the chance to disrupt the norm, he not only gained a new client, but he gained a friend. You can't be afraid to set yourself apart from your competition. You are your brand and you need to sell yourself before selling anything else.

What makes you want to buy from somebody?

I will use hairstylists as an example. Any hairstylist I've ever gone to was likely referred to me by a friend or family member. I never went to anyone that I was particularly unhappy with, but it did take me a long time to find a person who I would follow, no matter where he was working. Of all the entrepreneurs that I've known in my day, Thom Haraczy is one who takes branding himself as his niche to a level that is beyond imagination. His niche is that he not only has the ability to make you look beautiful on the outside, but when you leave him you feel beautiful on the inside. He invests himself in his clients by getting to know everything about you and remembering it, so that you're looking forward to your next visit with him.

It's fitting that he named his salon "Possibilities", because that's exactly what you feel your life has after the time you spend with him. My funeral-director friend Jack and my hairstylist Thom are making emotional connections with their clients. They exemplify the way Entrepreneur.com describes niche: "with whom do you want to do business?"

Next time you are going to dinner or paying for a service, think about what led you to choose that business. I'm guessing it is a business that identifies their niche and used it to market to you.

8

Network Equals Net Worth

*B*uilding a good network of people is essential when trying to create a lucrative business or career. You simply never know who you're going to meet and who they might know.

Growing your network means growing your net worth. Involve yourself with clubs and organizations where like-minded people show up for the very same reason. Always remember, it **is** who you know.

Early in my career, I remember being invited to different networking events. My partner and I would show up together and enter a room not knowing anybody. Nine out of ten times we ended up standing in the corner by ourselves, complaining that it was much like high school where you had little cliques of people. It was uncomfortable to say the very least.

Now let's fast forward several years later, to a time when we were starting to get to know other people in business because we were providing a service to them. Attending network events wasn't as painful as it once was, when we didn't know anybody in the room. But looking back, I have to admit that I probably looked like one of those people who was in a clique, because I was with other people that I already knew. I stayed close to those who I knew, because that was where my comfort zone was. That kind of networking was defeating the purpose, because the whole idea of going to different events was to get to know new people so that you broaden that base of contacts.

As you increase the number of people in your network you are increasing your opportunities. Matt Youngquist, the president of Career Horizons, points out that 70-80% of jobs are not even published, yet most people spend their time looking for work online thirty to forty hours per week (interviewed by Wendy Kaufman, February 3, 2011, https://www.npr.org/2011/02/08/133474431/a-successful-job-search-its-all-about-networking). Whether looking for a job or looking to build your client list, face to face contact gives you the leading edge. This can be summed up in the African proverb that says, "If you want to go fast, go alone. If you want to go far, go with others." If you are happy with turning on an "open for business" sign and waiting for success, sit behind your desk and wait. **If you want to be your best, get out and meet people who want the same for themselves as they want for you.**

The key is to surround yourself with those who are doing, not those who are watching. When I was young, inexperienced and somewhat arrogant, I thought that leaving my office during working hours would be detrimental to my business. Essentially, I was sitting at my desk waiting for clients to come to me rather than getting out from behind my desk and going to meet new clients.

When taking the time out of your work day to attend these kind of events, you are potentially putting yourself in front of multiple clients at the same time. It is said that every person you meet knows one hundred more people. So, while they may not have the immediate need for your services, if they get to know you, like you and trust you, then there will come a time that they will be referring you. When I finally caught on to this concept, I started to enjoy going to any networking event that I could possibly attend. I chose groups that made no secret that they were there because they intended to grow their sales and their business.

We live in a generation of referrals. How many times do you log onto your social media and you see a request for recommendations? Every time a person responds to those posts, you have the opportunity to be seen by many people, free of charge. Do keep in mind that if you don't provide a quality service or product, this can also work against you. People are quick to post bad experiences on social media, but not as apt to post the good experiences. Because I understand the value of networking and growing a business based on referrals, I will always share my good experiences.

Just this past month, I was given a social media referral for some landscaping work that I needed done. This was after having two companies that were no-show, no-call. In haste, I was going to draw attention to the failed companies, but remembered that a negative attitude yields negative outcomes. I was finally given a name through my new network in Florida. This man brought his two sons and did an absolutely fantastic job for me. As a sincere expression of gratitude, I took a picture of his business card and posted it on our community social media page, thanking him and his children for doing such a fantastic job. As you can imagine, there were several posts thanking me for the networking referral since there are too many companies that don't follow through.

You can't buy that kind of advertising. If you happen to be the one who is referred in this case, you can pretty much surmise that the person who is going to call you is prequalified, because they're taking the advice of somebody they trust. You can choose to spend thousands in advertising, which may yield a larger quantity of leads. But I would take quality leads over quantity any given day.

Several years ago, we had the unfortunate situation of a drunk driver driving through our office building. Immediately upon learning of this accident, our networking connections were put into action. The first call was a restoration company who would actually do the cleanup and secure the building. The second call was to an electrician who would cut the electric service to the building. Every contractor that we hired to take care of that unexpected situation were all business professionals that we had met through our networking groups. Again, they were people that we knew, liked and trusted.

Spending time with like-minded people in business gives you the opportunity to share your business experiences. Before I was involved in networking and knew so many people, if I had a question, I would have to go to the phone book and find a company or consultant who would charge me for even asking a question. Now I could go to my Rolodex full of business cards of local professionals I knew personally, and I could ask them how they would handle a specific situation. And I was always happy to reciprocate.

There eventually came a time when the networking part of my job was my favorite part of the job. It just seems that when you surround yourself with entrepreneurs, their energy is addictive. I'm not going to lie: when I first started to attend events, I probably didn't take it as seriously as I should have.

The first Thursday of every month, there was a meeting at six-thirty in the morning. I recall several times my alarm going off and looking out to see two feet of snow, and falling right back into bed until it was time to go and open the office. So, you can only imagine that after a year of giving it a half-hearted effort, when it came time to renew my membership I said to the people that ran the program that I wasn't really getting much out of it for the membership fee. The reality was I wasn't putting enough effort into it to be able to see a return on my investment. That was nobody's fault but my own.

I agreed to give it another year. The next year I had vowed that I was going to make the most of what the group had to offer. As the leader of the group, Phil Kerner used to tell people, "Donna Rae finally got it."

For many years prior to this, I was simply a woman who knew a thing or two about bugs and I could balance a checkbook. But after putting my heart into getting to know people and what they have to offer and what I have to offer them, I felt like a woman who could run the country.

Not only were these business people and entrepreneurs that I would exchange business ideas and referrals with, they were now becoming my inner circle of very good friends. Let's face it, the people that you choose to spend your time with will influence who you are and what you do. It makes both personal and business sense to surround yourself with people who have good attitudes and are positive and uplifting – people who want to celebrate your success along with you.

Opportunities also come from meeting like-minded people. Such opportunities could be joint ventures, partnerships, client leads, etc. Through my networking, I formed a very nice working and personal relationship with my competitors, Kelly and Doug Welser. We would not hesitate to refer each other's businesses if we were unable to fulfill a client request. At one point, we shared a centerfold article in a small business magazine about competition that worked well together.

Through my networking while writing this book, I was referred to a publisher who was putting together a book on inspiring women. Flatteringly, I was offered a chapter in that book. "Voices of the 21st Century" will be released about the same time as my own. Networking opened that door for me.

When choosing the group or groups that will fit best for you, I always suggest that you look for a group that gives you the opportunity to do what is referred to as your "elevator pitch" in front of the room at least once per month.

In my life, I never imagined that I'd be at a loss for words until I was standing with a microphone in front of one hundred people the first time I did this, and my tongue was tied. The first several meetings that I attended, I would write out a thirty-second commercial and I would practice it over and over in the mirror so as not to embarrass myself in front of other entrepreneurs. The more I did it, the more my confidence grew, the more comfortable I felt, and I couldn't wait until my turn in front of the microphone. Being comfortable speaking in front of and to strangers is very important because your growth relies on your ability to communicate well with others. I've seen some of the shyest people I know transform to an entirely new comfort zone by learning how to speak in front of a room.

No longer did I have to write a thirty-second speech and rehearse it for the fear of embarrassing myself in front of other people. I knew my business well enough to talk about it for hours at a time. Now I was comfortable enough in front of the other entrepreneurs that I could speak without being rehearsed.

Learning how to speak in front of a room definitely gave me the confidence when speaking to a new client. If you are lacking confidence, networking will definitely benefit in helping you learn to carry on a meaningful conversation with somebody you are just getting to know. Who would have ever imagined that this love for speaking would turn into my next career? I'm finding that the new generation of entrepreneurs is more focused on these social media platforms for their network building. But I firmly believe there is no comparison to good eye contact and a strong handshake.

I've mentioned throughout this chapter that you should join formal networking groups. Keep in mind that there are other ways of networking that are equally as effective. For some, that might mean getting involved with church activities. Or maybe you have young kids and getting involved with PTA will open doors to new opportunities. I was asked on several occasions, by entrepreneurs that I met through networking, to join them in volunteering for different nonprofit and charitable causes in our community. This was a win-win situation. The nonprofits were getting the help they desperately needed and those of us who were helping were rewarded by meeting all kinds of new people.

More recently, after moving out of state and knowing very few people, I stumbled across a social media network of neighborhood women who were in the same boat as I was. They had moved to Florida, mostly from the north, and were finding it difficult to meet new people. We decided that we would attempt to organize a dinner every six weeks or so to try and meet new people. It was such a hit the first time we got together, that in just over a month we've had a third group event and many adventures in between getting to know new friends. And while it started out as a neighborhood networking group, these dynamic women are supporting each other in new career endeavors, sharing contacts and simply acting as a support network to enhance each other's lives. The "Queens of Waterford Lakes" were born and I expect will carry on for generations to come. The power of networking goes far beyond a sales call.

No matter what avenue you choose to start building your inner circle of new contacts, always remember to listen first. Show a genuine interest in what a person has to offer. Always be ready to exchange information. Have your business card available at all times. I prefer to use business cards that have a photo included, as this is certainly effective in helping keep the name with the face. Call me old-fashioned, but I still believe that a handwritten thank you note, giving that personal touch, will give you greater credibility and appreciation.

An "open for business" sign will never yield growth like finding and building a good network.

9

Overcoming Roadblocks

We've all heard the line that when life gives you lemons, make lemonade. Your personal and professional lives will certainly come with roadblocks. How you choose to approach adversity will define you. Roadblocks can help empower you, and build character and confidence if you tackle them with a can-do attitude.

Have you ever known someone who, no matter what the circumstances are, will have fifty reasons why the situation will never improve? You can speak to these types of people until you're blue in the face, but they will continue to have a defeatist attitude.

If you want to succeed in anything, you can't be that person. Adversity exists everywhere. To resist it will only allow it to persist. Adversity is one of the biggest obstacles everyone is going to face at some point in their life. You need to realize that anything is possible. How we approach a roadblock will determine the outcome. Are you self-defeating or do you take the approach that the roadblock has presented itself simply to make you stronger?

My biggest challenge through the years always seemed to be somebody telling me that I couldn't do something. Rather than believing it, I always set out on a mission to prove them wrong. I wasn't going to let the attitudes of negative people get in the way of anything that I set out to do. Any time I was able to do something that somebody told me that I couldn't, the feeling of accomplishment was that much greater. Friedrich Nietzsche once said, "That which does not kill you makes you stronger." And I can attest to that because I'm living proof.

I wouldn't be telling the truth if I told you that I was one who always saw the bright side of things. I definitely wasn't that person early on. I didn't take criticism well, even if I was asking for somebody's honest opinion. My own nephew Shaun would lovingly refer to me as "Turbo". He was trying to point out that I would take a situation and amplify it ten times when it really wasn't that big a deal. I'm not sure to whom or what to attribute my change in attitude to, but the day I did was the day that much bigger and better things started happening for me.

Recently, while writing this book, I was having a conversation with some friends. I asked them what they thought their biggest challenges were, whether it was in their work or their personal life. They all agreed that they felt there just wasn't enough time in a day to do everything that needed to be done. I'm sure there has been a point in your life that you can probably relate to that. To help improve your time management, you need to be clear on what your goals are and that each day you're using your time effectively to help achieve those goals.

One of the greatest pieces of advice that I can lend you is that you need to learn how to say "no". This was a problem for me for a long time. I had a fear that if I said no to somebody that they wouldn't consider me for a project in the future or that they may somehow take it personally. My inability to say no was just creating that much more anxiety with my own time management roadblock. We all have the same hours in a day and learning how to use those hours effectively is imperative.

Besides, if you are saying "yes" when you should be saying "no", you will likely not put your best effort forward, and eventually it will cause frustration to not only you, but to those who enlisted your help.

A typical day for me started by putting dinner in the crock pot at five-thirty in the morning then getting myself ready for work. Not only did I have my own two boys to care for, we were a host family to two teenage OHL hockey players for nine months of the year.

Next, I had to get boys up and ready for the day. In order to help with my own time management, I taught my sons how to be independent at a very early age: in elementary school they were making their own breakfast, and by the time they were in eighth grade they were doing their own laundry. Not only did this allow me more time to focus on building my business, it was teaching them responsibility. If time management becomes an issue for you, don't be afraid to ask for help from your friends and family.

When my kids were young they wanted to play hockey, and anyone who knows that sport knows there is an incredible time commitment. Their dad and I could have been selfish and told them, no, it's not possible, because we're running two businesses and trying to grow them to provide them with the things that they wanted.But if they wanted to make the commitment to play hockey, then we were going to commit to them to find a way. We enlisted the help of my brother, Doug, who was more than happy to help tote them from rink to rink.

I always lived by the fact that where there is a will there is a way. Another roadblock that I tend to create for myself is not learning how to delegate properly. I had the attitude that if you want something done right you need to do it yourself. Whether you want success in your home or in a business, you need to trust that the people that you surround yourself with can be as capable as you are if given the chance. **Delegating tasks to others will afford you the time and the opportunity to focus on bigger and better things.**

Another obstacle that many people talk about running into is not having enough money. Let's take a quick look at some of the contributing factors. Firstly, do you live and work by a budget? In either your home or a business, you need to be clear about what your income and your expenses are. You're certain to get yourself into trouble if you don't know those basics.

Another area where I see people get themselves into trouble is using credit cards without the ability to pay them back, or even by taking an extra $50,000 in a new mortgage simply because the lender offered it. Suddenly, they find that when they go to sell their house the value doesn't equal the equity.

One of the greatest lessons my mother taught us was the value of a credit score. During a recent coaching session I had with Antonio Smith Jr, he offered an analogy that I thought was simply brilliant. Antonio said, "Your credit score is a numerical map of your character." Right away I posted that quote on my Facebook page, because I think that too many people don't understand the value of a credit score.

Of course, as expected, I had some immediate opposition. I understand that it might not be as black and white as that and sometimes there are circumstances beyond a person's control. But I also know that anyone that I know that has ever had a bad credit score will never take ownership of it. You need to learn to budget and live within your means. You should never use a credit card for more than a thirty-day interest-free loan. Do not ever live by the theory of spend now and worry about how to pay it back later. Better financial planning will help you to avoid a future of financial roadblocks.

There was a point in the early stages of business that I had maxed out at least four credit cards. Those were the days before I understood how important it was to live and work on a budget. There is a big difference between needs and wants. Your needs take priority, your wants are earned after your income exceeds your expenses.

Ironically, it was that kind of lecture to local politicians that eventually ended up getting me elected.

The other area where people tend to get themselves in trouble is not putting away money as a rainy-day fund. While I was serving on the school board, I approved some small tax increases to help our district build our reserve. I was surprised at the number of people on social media posts that would criticize this decision. I often posed the question back to them: if you own a home and you don't have money in savings, what are you going to do when your roof is leaking, and you have no money to repair it?

Unless you're fortunate enough to inherit a home or a business where you have no financial obligation to pay for it, then it is a must to learn how to be smart with your money. There are people that I've known over the years who thought that because we were in a generational family business that it must have just simply landed in our laps free of charge. That couldn't be further from the truth.

When Jim and I first purchased the business, we were both working full-time, yet neither one of us was coming home with a paycheck because every dime that we had was either paying for the business or covering our expenses. We still needed to pay our mortgage and our household expenses. That meant that one of us had to work after hours and one of us would have to be home with our older son Ryan. We agreed that Jim would stay home with Ryan and I would go waitress nights and weekends.

Having this kind of time and financial obligation certainly lit a fire with us to grow our business so that we didn't have to have this kind of schedule. It took about a year before I was able to quit the second job because we were generating enough from our own business to now pay ourselves. We finally had some breathing room.

I don't consider what happened next to be a roadblock, but it certainly did test our abilities to adjust to unexpected circumstances. We received news from our doctor that we were now expecting our second child and that child was due at the beginning of our very busiest season. We spent the next several months preparing and planning so that we were ready to meet the needs of both our new child as well as our new clients.

On Friday, April 3rd our son Shane was born and on Monday morning, I was right back in our office, baby in tow. This was another time in my life where people around me told me that there was no way possible that I was going to make this work. I'm not going to fool you into thinking that it was easy, but anything worthwhile is worth putting your best foot forward.

That was twenty-six years ago and we still have customers who ask how that baby is, only to find out that that baby and his brother are now the fourth-generation working owners of that business.

Roadblocks will only stop you if you let them. It is up to you to program your brain not to react to a situation, but to act only after you've taken the time to evaluate and come up with a feasible plan.

I've now talked about two subjects that most people can identify with at one point or another: lack of time and lack of money.

With both of those subjects, you have the ability to take control of both.

Have you ever sat and imagined what it would be like if you received an unfavorable medical diagnosis? That's not something that most of us sit around and plan for, at least I didn't. In 2002 I received devastating news that I was suffering from degenerative disc disease. Whether you're working for somebody or you're self-employed, there is never a good time for that kind of diagnosis. I chose to do what many A-type entrepreneur personalities would do, and I put off any kind of treatment for several years, only compounding the problem.

In order to be the best version of yourself, you need to take care of your health first. My decision to ignore it eventually led to an emergency fusion. Five surgeries in two years and two neurosurgeons later, I was living with unmanageable pain daily that was affecting every area of my life.

At the same time, I was given a diagnosis of Interstitial Lung Disease, which can eventually become terminal without a lung transplant. I was basically being told that my life was over at the age of forty-nine. The decision was made, it was time to sell my shares of the business to my sons and relocate to Florida for treatment where the year-round warm weather was so much better for my condition.

This certainly was never part of my business plan. I went through a great deal of time where I did nothing but sit and wallow in self-pity. I certainly never looked sick from the outside, which posed a whole new set of challenges from the number of people in my life who would judge me. I had a family member one day suggest that maybe if I went to the gym I would feel better. I was allowing not only the outside negative voices get to me, but my own negative voices were starting to take control.

One day while unpacking in Florida, I stumbled across my copy of *The Secret*. I found myself going to the chapter on health over and over again. There are examples of people who were literally cured of cancer. And a story of a man who had wrecked his plane and overheard the doctors saying that he was going to be in a vegetative state for life. He talks about how he programmed his brain that he would walk out of the hospital eight months later on Christmas Day, and he did exactly that.

That day was it for me. I was tired of feeling sorry for myself. I started to research my condition and I found a doctor in Orlando who was able to offer me hope for managing my chronic pain. I knew that I needed something to look forward to that would help create a positive focus. I tapped back into my entrepreneurial spirit and I looked at what I could do in Orlando so that I could set yet another lofty goal of working again after being told by multiple medical professionals that that would never happen for me.

As fate would have it, while doing research on the Internet, one day a website popped up that said, "You have a story." The stars were definitely aligned for me that day because when I clicked on the link it took me right to the Les Brown Institute. I don't think it's a coincidence that I was now having the opportunity to professionally train with my favorite motivational speaker of all time from the comfort of my own home. The lesson that I learned here is that of all the organs in your body, your mind is the most powerful. Frank Clark said it best, "If you can find a path with no obstacles, it probably doesn't lead anywhere."

Life is going to come with obstacles. Don't let it be the end of your world. **Change your thinking, and it will change your life.**

10
Changing Direction

*W*ealth doesn't happen by accident.

Wanting more, setting large goals and being determined to work smarter, not harder, is the answer to a lifetime of financial freedom. Being hungry helps drive you to do everything you need to achieve financial success. Financial success is not just being able to cover your bills or your debt, it's knowing that you can have what you want, when you want it and that you won't have to work until the day you die.

Would you sleep better at night if you weren't worrying about how to meet your financial obligations? Wouldn't you rather go to bed at night knowing that you were getting up the next day to go on a luxury seven-day cruise because money isn't an obstacle? Recently I overheard somebody say that people who claim that money doesn't buy happiness never had any money. I don't know a person on this earth who doesn't secretly want more, but are likely feeling guilty about it because changes in society today may make you feel selfish if you believe that you should have more, even if you work harder for it.

I was eight-years-old and working on the farm when I realized how much I enjoyed the fruits of my labor. My very reason for writing this book and sharing my experiences is to show you that, no matter what your circumstances may be, you can have anything and be anything that you set your mind to.

Do you remember the Occupy Wall Street 99% movement of August 2011? There were protests about income inequality in the US, due to the concentration of wealth being among the top 1% income earners. Given the opportunity, what percentage would you want to fall in? The 1%ers or the 99%?

While in Washington DC for a business conference, I witnessed hundreds, if not thousands of people camped out with tents and chairs in nearly every piece of open lawn. It was perplexing to me to think that they were able to spend twenty-four hours a day, for weeks at a time to protest that people like me had more than they did.

My first thought was that if they put forth that kind of time and effort into making money as they did protesting, there would be more than 1% in the highest income category. While walking along the mall area, it was hard not to notice that they were observing me, just as I was observing them. I told the person that I was with that I would love nothing more than to interview a few of these people to get a better understanding of their mindset.

What was it that made them believe that income should somehow be equal if the effort isn't? They were choosing to spend their time complaining about those who work tirelessly their whole life to achieve success and somehow think they deserve the same without putting forth the same effort. Opportunity is available to anyone who wishes to work for it.

I read a startling statistic that says the majority of people in this country cannot afford a $400 emergency. I've known many people that fall into this category. I also understand why many ended up as part of that statistic. Most people aren't looking and planning ahead, but rather, living in the moment, content with living paycheck to paycheck. Many are like people that use more energy on excuses than actions to improve their situation.

What would you do if you had a real life tragedy? In 2013 this is exactly what happened for me. Without going into details, my home sustained nearly $100,000 in damages. I was without a home, and forced to live out of a hotel room for a period of time. Insurance would not cover the damages because it wasn't from an accident or Act of God. I had to resort to my retirement savings to restore my home to livable conditions.

Strangers who saw my story in our local news would often stop me and ask how I was able to survive this tragedy. Had I not had money in the bank, what would have happened? A bank isn't going to give an equity loan on a home with this much damage. Had I not been strict about saving, that incident would have likely left me bankrupt and homeless. Eventually, nearly four years and a lot of attorney's fees later, I was able to recover the damages. The stress and anxiety throughout that four-year period was incredibly hard to handle at times.

It's never a good idea as an entrepreneur to have all your eggs in one basket. Whether you own a business or you're employed by a business, in addition to having more than one revenue source, it's always very important to put a portion of everything you earn away. It might be for a rainy day or for your retirement.

Do you ever think about what you would do if you got fired from a job? Or in my case, was diagnosed with a chronic health problem that forced an early retirement, and went through a catastrophic loss with my home? Being disciplined with the money you do have only creates more money.

My entire life I had a fear of what would happen if I ran out of money, which made me that much more hungry to make and save more. It is also that mindset that encouraged me to think outside of the box on how to make money again in spite of physical limitations. You are never too old to recreate yourself. It doesn't matter what age you are at this very moment; if you are not where you want to be financially, then take the action to change it!

Too many operate under the notion that the wealthiest people were born into it and didn't have to work for it. But I already gave several examples of people who were born destitute who made their way into millions and billions. You hold the key to unlocking your unlimited wealth. The only thing holding you back is you.

When I finished high school, I wasn't sure what I wanted to do with my future. My sister had taken a one-year course caring for people with disabilities. I was so touched by it that I thought, maybe I'll just do the same thing. After completing that course, I had to weigh the option of going into the workforce on a nurse's aide's wage or enrolling in college to get a degree that would allow greater earning potential. Since I was always motivated by money, I chose to enroll in college. I was now a nineteen-year-old broke college student and I didn't take being broke well at all.

After only one year of college, I dropped out and took a teacher's aide job in a school for children with disabilities. At age twenty I got married and my husband and I were able to buy a starter home after being given a small gift of a down payment by his grandparents. In 1985, the first year we were married, our combined income was only $20,000 and we were both working full-time. I was not content at all with just being able to pay our mortgage and our car payment, having no money left at the end of the week. I also knew that being a teacher's aide was not going to provide me with financial advancement in my future. After working my eight-hour day I enrolled in evening classes at a business school with the intention of eventually moving into an office job that would allow me the opportunity of advancement. At the same time, I took on babysitting jobs and started videotaping weddings, anything that I could do to make more money.

My husband and I knew that the day would eventually come when his father retired and would sell the family pest control company to us. Of course, being young and naïve, with no business experience, we thought we would walk right into a business and be rolling in dough. The day finally came when we bought the business. The overhead of the purchase as well as the everyday business expenses was draining us. We were broke again. I'm embarrassed to admit that I was once one of those people who thought that if you owned a business, you worked less than anybody else and had more. My husband and I were both working the business full-time, but neither of us were collecting a paycheck. I had no other option than to go to work a second job to pay our personal bills. The only way that we were going to make money off the business that we were buying was to grow it.

This was a lot of weight for a couple in their early twenties who had nothing but a high school education and a toddler at home. If I had not been driven by the desire to make more money, it would have been easy to become a victim and throw in the towel. Many of our friends at the time were graduating college and were enjoying professional wages at nine-to-five jobs. For a short time, I regretted quitting college and envied the lives that my friends were now leading.

Thank goodness that regret was short-lived. Most nine-to-five jobs are a fixed salary where if lucky, you may get a three percent cost of living increase annually. I wanted more, and I wanted it now. The changes that we had been making to the family business were now starting to pay off. Our growth was phenomenal and now so was the money that we were starting to take home. By age twenty-nine we were buying a second business. The days of having ulcers from stress and sleepless nights over money were definitely a thing of the past. The more money I made, the more money I wanted. Fortunately, years later, I was in a more secure financial position and was able to offer annual contributions to people with disabilities, through the very non-profit where I had obtained my nurse aid certification.

Most successful entrepreneurs have multiple streams of income. Even before buying our first business, when we were new homeowners, we rented our spare bedroom to a college student for added income. We made a business decision to sell the business property that had been in the family for years. We were able to downsize to a property that had equal visibility as well as a rental unit connected to it. We were now in a building on which we had no loan and we were receiving additional income from the rental side of it.

I've gone through periods of my life where I act as if I am stone broke when, in reality, I have more in savings than some earn in a lifetime. My boys used to question me about that before they were running a business. Being a seasonal business means that the bulk of your revenue is made in only six months out of the year. That means being disciplined enough to take those revenues and put them away to sustain you during the time that the revenue is little to nothing. Financial obligations don't disappear when your income does.

Having to budget like that in the business also provided discipline in my personal life. After divorcing, I was down to one income and still had all the household and personal expenses. I was able to maintain the life that I was accustomed to because of the discipline practiced when there were two incomes in the household.

Also, keep in mind that when you're self-employed, there is no employer contribution to your retirement savings. You are solely responsible for your own retirement which means saving money is imperative. Social Security retirement earnings could never sustain a household alone.

Rather than sitting back in envy over those with more, I adopted the mindset that I wanted to be just like them. At forty-nine years old, due to my chronic illness, I had to make the decision to retire early and sell my share of the business to my sons. I never imagined that I would be without an income at such a young age.

However, there was a bright side. I had saved for a rainy day and it was raining hard. I will be the first to admit that life was more than an adjustment. I had finally got myself to the point where I didn't have to worry one bit how I was spending money, because there was plenty coming in and there was plenty saved.

But in the blink of an eye, that all changed. I now understood what senior citizens meant when they said that they couldn't afford things because they were now on a fixed income. Not knowing the fate of my future due to illness, I had to start living very cautiously so that I didn't outlive my savings. It didn't take me long of being on a fixed income to figure out that that was not going to be my future. It was time to recreate myself and set new financial goals around my limitations.

I sought treatment in Florida where the weather was so much better for my condition but the trip back and forth from Erie to Pittsburgh was just too hard on me. I was literally starting every aspect of my life over, and not by choice.

I researched job sites regularly to see where I could utilize my years of business experience, while praying for the day that I would start to see improved health. I was reading books by authors like Rhonda Byrne, Les Brown and Zig Ziglar to help maintain a positive attitude when I wasn't feeling very positive at all. I chose books about overcoming adversity and building wealth, always focusing on my favorite line from *The Secret*, that thoughts become things.

On April 4th of 2017, I felt as though I was hit by a bolt of lightning. I realized I had a story and that my story of overcoming adversity and creating wealth might just be the answer to what I had been looking for. It was that day that I started writing this book. I knew that what I had experienced throughout my lifetime could help inspire others. Coincidentally, just days later when Googling the keywords "how to tell your story", Les Brown's website popped up. I added yet another goal for myself, to become formally certified under Les as a motivational speaker and corporate coach/trainer. I was no longer sweating about the possibility of outliving my savings. I had set clear goals and immediately went to work on action plans to achieve them. As Montel Williams stated after his medical diagnosis, "Mountain, get out of my way!"

You have to choose for yourself and it starts by wanting something badly enough that you'll do whatever it takes to get it. Do you want to be the person who is broke, buying lottery tickets in the hopes of being one out of 292 million to hit the millions? Or does it make better sense to invest your time and money in yourself where your return on investment is unlimited?

I stumbled across an anonymous quote for the people out there who have everything but want more. It simply reads: "very nice, but does that come in black?"

11
Living Your Best Life

$\mathcal{I}$n the previous chapters of this book, I talked about different angles of how you can utilize your time, how you can get results faster and also the importance of learning from your failures. Of all the chapters in the book, this one sheds the most light on how to make the most ordinary life an amazing one. You have to realize that you're in the driver's seat of your life. **What road you choose to take is nobody's choice but yours.**

The single most powerful word that changed everything for me is the word "gratitude". If you want to control the outcomes of things that happen in your life, you need to control your vibration. If everything that you put out is negative, negative is what you're going to get in return. Most people are living in reverse, by allowing outside influences to become their outcome.

When you begin to start each day grateful for what you already have, doors of opportunity opening will be endless. It took me losing my livelihood as well as tragic personal losses to fully understand that my lack of gratitude may have placed limitations on me and slowed down my success. When

I refer to success I'm not just talking monetarily, I'm talking success in relationships as well. Happiness is an inside job. If you're anything like what I used to be and continually look for the approval of those around you versus what makes you happy, then you're only placing unnecessary limitations on you yourself.

Both the word satisfaction and attraction end with the keyword "action". So as the driver of your destiny, what road do you choose? The long, dark, narrow road or the one that is nicely paved and very smooth sailing? I'm not proud having to share in this chapter that I was often a very difficult person to live and work with. I was never fully aware of the extent, nor the reasons that I could be so difficult, until I started reading books by great motivators, because I was lacking motivation myself.

I had myself convinced that my misery was the fact that I had to wake up living with chronic pain each day. I was constantly looking for any reason other than the sheer fact that I was a miserable person. One day it hit me like a brick. Les Brown said, "Someone's opinion of you does not have to become your reality." Those words had a deep impact and were essential in helping me understand that if improvements to my life were going to be made, they had to start with me.

This brings me to the importance of having healthy relationships in order to be the best at anything you want to be. The first and most important relationship is the one that you have with yourself. When you learn to love yourself first, you become a magnet to positive people and influence. My healing wasn't just happening emotionally, but it was happening physically too. I was feeling better all the way around as a result of a change in my attitude. How can you ever expect to bring out the best in others if you haven't brought out the best in yourself first?

You will always be lonely if you're relying on others for your happiness. If you are always miserable, it's because you are focusing on things that didn't go right in your past, rather than focusing on the good that's happening in the present. You can't rewrite your book in the past, nor can you predict the future, but you can certainly live each day in the present. It's time for you to decide that your dreams are necessary. You can start to realize your dreams when you release the thoughts of having limitations. Some of my darkest days came as a result of people in the medical profession telling me that I was going to have limitations put on me long before I ever expected them.

My biggest regret is that for a long time I listened to them. This created doubt about everything that I was doing. I was finding it difficult to go to work and last through the day, because I was told that I couldn't.

As strong as I once was, I was now questioning my ability to serve in a publicly-elected seat by allowing small-minded individuals the ability to take advantage of my weakness. Because I was focusing on negative thoughts, I was attracting negative people into my life. When things are going badly for you, the only way to change your outlook is to consider people who are worse off. Not long after starting treatment in Florida, I was introduced to a gentleman who showed me a different perspective.

The man was eighty-nine years old and had recently lost the wife that he had married when only nineteen. It didn't matter how bad he was feeling, he always met you with a smile and the biggest hug that would light up your day. Not long after I met John, he was diagnosed with terminal cancer. Doctors projected that he had three-to-six months to live, with or without treatment. John decided for himself that if there was a remote chance that treatment might help, even if it changed the quality of his life, he was going to try anything. My days of feeling sorry for myself were over. I had a friend whose situation was far worse than I could ever imagine mine to be, yet he wasn't feeling sorry for himself.

Keeping in mind that he was told that he could have as little as three months left to live, those closest to him knew him well enough that he would want to make the best of any time he was given. One night, after taking him to karaoke, he very cheerfully told me, "I will not let this beat me." It was close to the three-month period of the diagnosis when I took him for a PET scan. Amazingly, he was not showing any signs of illness, even from the weekly chemo treatments he was having. On the way home from the PET scan, I asked him if there was anything that he had left to do that he hadn't yet done. He responded by chuckling and saying what? My bucket list? Being eighty-nine and having lived a fulfilling life, he only had a couple of requests, one of which was going to Cape Canaveral to watch the cruise ships leave the port. Just four days later, John, myself and twelve of his closest friends spent the most amazing and memorable day ever, fulfilling his bucket list requests.

It was one day later that his daughter and my dear friend, Teal, took him to his follow up appointment for the PET scan results. John was right, cancer wasn't going to beat him. His PET scan results came back and he was completely clear of any cancer.

According to studies done by the Harvard T.H. Chan School of Public Health, people who lead more optimistic lives significantly reduced their risk of dying from diseases such as cancer, stroke and heart disease, over those who were more pessimistic ("Happiness & health", Winter 2011, http://www.hsph.harvard.edu). John turned ninety-one this past February and is more active than most thirty-year-olds I know. John's overwhelmingly positive attitude not only saved his life, but I truly believed helped save mine.

If you were told that you had three to six months to live, would you be living your life the same as you are right now?

It took the tragic loss of my sisters to fully wake me up.

Just over a year ago I got a call that one of my five sisters was in the hospital just an hour away from my Florida home. I rushed to her bedside to find out that she had been diagnosed with stage four bone cancer. She wanted us to move her north so that she could be surrounded by our family. We made the arrangements and had her moved immediately. Sadly, she passed away just five weeks later. Now let's fast forward four months later, I received yet another call that my older sister Deedee, who was more like a mom to me, was in an ambulance, unresponsive. She had had an aneurysm. I was unable to get a flight out until morning and my family decided to pull her off life support that night.

My sister Dorey held the phone next to Deedee's ear as I sobbed, and I begged her to wait for her daughter and me to get there, so we could be present for her final breath. She defied all medical rationale and waited for us. Both my sisters went to their graves with unrealized dreams. Jane was hoping to open a bait and tackle business on a small lake in Florida. Deedee had worked her entire life, raised six kids and was hoping to spend her retirement travelling.

Each of them had negative people in their lives who played a role in holding them back. Their tomorrows never came. Like the lesson that I learned from John who decided to live his life in spite of what doctors were telling him, I learned an equal lesson from my sisters, to live each and every day as if it were your last, because tomorrow is not promised. In spite of losing my brother Dennis to cancer and my two sisters, I still have a big family. After these losses my sister Dorey started to evaluate her own life, just as I have. She also took the necessary steps to remove the negative energy from her life and is now spending more and more time not only getting to know what her own value and purpose is, but spending time with her son who never lost faith in her abilities when she had.

Michael J. Fox once summed it up when he said, "Family is not an important thing. It's everything." Family aren't just those with your bloodline, but also close friends. **It is important for you to surround yourself with people who see your vision and honor it just as if it were their own.**

When I was a young entrepreneur I used to think that wealth was the amount of money and objects that you could gain in a lifetime. But my greatest wealth never came in the form of money or things. It came with the birth of my sons, Ryan and Shane. I was now measuring my riches not in the form of the dollars that I could provide them, but rather the knowledge, the wisdom and the lessons that I could teach them so that they too would become respectful and productive adults. My role as a teacher to my own children was the greatest leadership role I've held in a lifetime. I also taught my kids the lesson that my mother taught me about the old adage, you are only as good as the company that you keep. They both had periods of their life when they may have resented me when they thought I was choosing their friends. Now that they are adults and working hard towards their own success they have a greater understanding of what I was trying to accomplish as their teacher and their parent.

By helping eliminate some of the bad influences in their early years, it helped them make better choices as young adults and they can look back now and see where they are, versus those who didn't have that kind of guidance. But my boys will tell you that there was a period of time where I lost focus and that I should have taken my own advice. I had taught them to become better judges of character than I had been myself.

Today it's somewhat hard to stay positive in a truly negative world.

While there may be tremendous business benefits to having social media, when it comes to a marketing vantage point in business it's also becoming increasingly difficult to maintain a good working attitude with such negative daily postings. In January of this year I woke up to the news of a federal government shutdown. My first mistake was turning on the TV. The second, even greater mistake, was signing onto social media. The pure hatred and finger pointing that was taking place by people that I once respected on both sides of the political fence was simply overwhelming. I wouldn't have expected that behavior from my kids as toddlers, let alone so-called educated adults. If my children had acted that way, I would have disciplined them for acting like bullies. The negativity that day had me so overwhelmingly frustrated, that I decided that twenty-four hours later that I was going to remove my Facebook account altogether. I made a final post telling people how they could reach me and why I would no longer be present on social media.

During our days in hockey we learned what was referred to as the 24-hour rule. That would be when a coach or a referee made a decision that was so upsetting to you that you would verbally attack them. The 24-hour rule said that if you still felt that way at the same time the following day, then it could be addressed. Nine out of ten times you take a deep breath and realize some things you simply can't change and it's not worth losing sleep over.

I implemented the 24-hour rule on my Facebook post. Why should I give up hundreds of people that I keep in regular contact with, people whose posts add value to my day, over a handful of very bitter people who, if they're not complaining about a political decision, they're complaining about something else every single day?

The following day I scrolled through the post and for every negative post, no matter if it was politically-motivated or not, I deleted the person as a Facebook friend. I even made a very difficult decision in deleting one of my very best friends. I wasn't getting rid of him as a friend, but I was getting rid of the negativity that people find so comfortable throwing out on social media. I sent him a text and explained to him that while I will always love him as one of my best friends, I cannot continue to read negative comments and think that somehow my life is going to have a positive outcome. We keep in regular contact, but the subject matter is on upbeat and positive subjects and our relationship has strengthened as a result.

Success in life can absolutely be achieved faster when you not only maintain a good attitude, but also surround yourself by those live with it also. There is the old saying that misery loves company. The day that I decided that that kind of company was no longer welcome was the changing point for me. Another significant thing I learned through reading books by accomplished individuals, was that in order to accelerate your success you need to practice forgiveness. Not only do you have to forgive yourself for your past mistakes, you cannot carry grudges and think that good things will come to you. If you constantly carry negative thoughts about someone because they once did you wrong, you will, by the laws of nature, attract more negative energy from others. Learn forgiveness and make a conscious effort to see the good in others.

My son came to me when he was in elementary school, bothered about some kids who were making fun of a classmate. I raised my kids to understand that when others choose to make fun of someone, it is because they don't feel good about themselves. This doesn't just apply to the behavior of children, I've encountered it as an adult, especially when holding a publicly-elected position.

It is getting to the point that in order to me for start my day with a positive attitude and maintain it, I need to ignore the television, radio and newspaper. How often are you hearing stories of success where people are actually celebrating instead of criticizing? What are we teaching the next generations, by allowing constant disdain for our leaders and educators? Is it any wonder that we've seen an increase in school violence, when misery is being taught over hard work and compassion?

Positive results have to begin with positive attitudes. Charles R. Swindoll once said, "Attitude is more important than the past, than education, than money, than circumstances, than what people do or say."

Start today.

12

Tenfold Returns

*Y*ou are an opening for the universe. It is up to you if you choose to start each day with every reason that things will go wrong. When you find gratitude and start giving your gift of time or money to others the universe will respond with tenfold returns.

Les Brown says, "I will heighten my life by helping others heighten theirs." No matter what our circumstances in life happen to be, each of us has something positive that we are able to offer to others. Giving doesn't have to be monetary.

While we don't all have the same amount of money, we are each given the gift of time. Whether it is a dream of becoming a successful entrepreneur or just improving your personal life, when you give yourself up to it, the law of attraction will be at work turning all the "why nots" in your life into "what can I do for you?" Suddenly you will find that your life will bring new meaning, you'll build stronger relationships and you will have greater fulfilment in everything that you do.

If you're at a position in your life where you're not feeling worthy of yourself, you certainly will not be able to help others.

Years ago, there was a call at our gift shop. The gentleman on the other end of the phone claimed to be calling from Iraq from a satellite phone. One of my staff thought that I should probably take that call. As it turned out, I had an active duty soldier on the other end of the line who was calling to place a cookie gift order to send to his wife who was battling breast cancer and raising his two young children.

Those children were at home with a sick mother while their dad was half a world away fighting for our country. After he placed the order he told me that he had his credit card number ready for me. I told him, "You can't pay me for this or any other order that you place with this business for the rest of your life. Anyone who puts his life on the line to protect me and my children has credit with me. Your bill is paid in full." From that day forward, anything that he needed from me was on the house.

I could not thank this soldier enough for what he was sacrificing on behalf of protecting our country and our freedoms. Nearly a year later, a gentleman came into my office and asked me if he could speak to Donna Rae. When I told him that I was her, he reached out to shake my hand and introduced himself as First Sergeant Bill Krawczyk. I was given the honor of shaking the hand of the soldier who had called my store many months earlier.

Sadly, Bill wasn't home because it was the end of his duty. He was home because he was now battling unexplained illnesses. My first question to him was, "How can I help?" What they needed the most from me were connections that I had made through years in business and my involvement in the political realm. I reached out to others I knew could help.

Within days of meeting him, my friends from the TV did a feature story on Bill. Our local newspaper also did a full-page cover story. Donations for a benefit started pouring in, along with several offers of help. For the next several months, the Krawczyk's and I were joined at the hip. I could never have imagined that a simple act of kindness in offering free cookie arrangements for a soldier would end up being one of my greatest blessings. The Krawczyk's and I have built a lifelong friendship.

There have been people I have encountered in life who have turned down opportunities to help someone in need because they say that people don't appreciate them.

What you have to realize is that giving to others is giving back to you. You must be the message. Are you grateful for what you have? Or what you're looking to get? My mother is the one I need to thank for teaching me the importance of giving to others without expecting anything in return. I never did quite understand how you could do things for some people and they just weren't grateful.

My mother taught me not to do things looking for a reward. She always reminded me that rewards only come in heaven. The question was, did I feel better at the end of the day when I was able to offer assistance to somebody who was in need? The answer is a wholehearted "yes", whether the person receiving my help was grateful or not.

If you want to see real success, it starts the very moment that you start giving back: it is the very foundation of having a successful life. You might already be thinking; how can you possibly be a successful entrepreneur, which takes so much time in the day to run your own business, *and* be involved with your community at the same time? My answer would be the old adage that if you want something done and you want it done right, ask a busy person. Highly successful people find the balance because they know that in the end, everybody wins.

In 2010, the ABC hit TV show *Extreme Home Makeover* came to my hometown. Business owners were flocking to the TV station to sign up, hoping to volunteer their goods and services to this project. My partner was able to secure our pest control company the honor of providing the termite pretreatment for the new home. It was overwhelming to have the opportunity to be part of such of an event.

Our company donated upwards of $5,000 in service and materials, while other companies donated ten times that amount. To come together with other local businesses on this charitable project is a memory that we will always have. We helped improve the lives of not only the recipient of the home, but an entire neighborhood that our community revitalized in five short days. The returns for us, besides the gratitude of being involved, were the relationships we formed with other volunteers – relationships that still exist today. Each and every entrepreneur on the project had a complete understanding of the importance of giving back.

One of the most brilliant fundraising events that I was asked to participate in was the Leukemia and Lymphoma Foundation. There was competition among a handful of local entrepreneurs. We were given several weeks for each of us to find creative ways to raise money. The one who raised the most money at the end of the competition would be named the Woman of the Year.

Creating a competition among entrepreneurs was genius. It should come as no surprise that all my competition were friends that I had met through networking. This challenge fell during the busiest time of the year for me. I didn't want to lose, but I also knew that my competition had the edge by being able to manage their time better. This was when my tenacious side kicked in yet again. I needed to work smarter, not harder, to raise money for this incredibly worthy foundation.

Coincidentally, at the very time that I was asked to help raise money on behalf of cancer research, my brother was battling his own cancer. He lost his battle just one week prior to the conclusion of our competition. I didn't want to focus on the negative aspects of cancer for my fundraising efforts. That's when it dawned on me that my son's girlfriend of many years was a cancer survivor. I enlisted the help of a friend, who I'd met through my networking, to make a professional video for me that I would then use on social media.

I shared Kelli's story about how she was a young child who wasn't supposed to survive cancer, and not only did she survive it, but she was now in a Division 1 college on an athletic scholarship. Being able to share an uplifting story of survival like Kelli's, I was able to show that the money that goes to research definitely saves lives. I didn't win the competition of Woman of the Year. I was able to raise $11,000 with the help of a video and the story of an amazing girl who had touched so many lives.

At the banquet, when the Woman of the Year was named, we all agreed that each and every one of us were winners, because the efforts we had put forth to raise money for the Leukemia and Lymphoma Foundation would help save lives.

Winston Churchill once said "We make a living by what we get, we make a life by what we give." I have to share that while writing this chapter, I got choked up several times along the way. The opening lines of this chapter state that you are an opening for the universe, and sharing the two stories that were very personal to me, made me realize that the help that was being asked from me in both those instances likely wasn't by accident. I am far richer from the memories that I have from those two experiences than any amount of money that I've ever earned.

"It's better to give than receive" is something we've all heard at one time or another. The fact is, in giving you will be receiving. Anything you give more of, it comes back tenfold. Whether it is giving more in your personal relationships, or offering help to strangers, the law of the universe has determined that your life or circumstances will improve without question.

In John F. Kennedy's inaugural address he made a statement that has been carried on for generations. He said "Ask not what your country can do for you, ask what you can do for your country." He challenged every American citizen to contribute what they could to help make our country a better place. Earl Nightingale said it best when he said "Our success in life is directly related to the quantity and quality of the service that we give."

According to research done by Harvard Business School, giving money to somebody else actually makes you feel better than spending it on yourself (*The Harvard Gazette*, April 17, 2008). Those who participated in the study had projected the opposite result. Another study done by Stony Brook University showed that when you are giving your brain releases chemicals that make you feel physically better. It was given the name "giver's glow." When you have the giver's glow, you attract positive people (Elizabeth Renter, May 1, 2015, http://health.usnews. com). And a study at Carnegie Mellon found that people who volunteer an average of four hours per week are 40% less likely to develop high blood pressure (Carnegie Mellon University Press Release, June 13, 2013, http://www.cmu.edu).

Christmas season has always been a very special time of year for me. When people say they don't like it because it increases their stress levels, I can never understand that. But after reading the outcome of these college studies on giving, it is no wonder my mood improves. I love giving.

My sons used to cringe when I wanted to put the Christmas tree up before Thanksgiving. Each year it seems that the decorations go up earlier and earlier. This has become my excuse to start giving sooner. I'm not alone in my obsession any longer. My son's darling girlfriend, Alexis, won my heart instantly with her attitude of gratitude in giving. She understands wholeheartedly the impact of offering random acts of kindness, not only to the person receiving, but for her also. Just this past winter, I told her about a woman I know who is battling cancer and losing her hair. Money was tight and she needed warm headwear for the trips back and forth to the cancer center. Alexis, who had never met this woman, went into action to find out what her favorite color was and loaded a box full of hats, scarves and mittens as a simple gesture. Alexis will tell you that the gift was truly hers, as the two have a special bond to this day.

There is further scientific research that says that giving causes a ripple effect (Jill Suttie & Jason Marsh, December 13, 2010, http://www.greatergood.berkeley.edu). An act of generosity could actually cause hundreds of people to do the same, which leads me to my next example.

In September of 2013, a young couple, Sarah and Jason O'Neill, tragically lost their daughter Alyssa to an epileptic seizure. The night before Alyssa's passing, she told her mom that she wanted to go to Starbuck's the following day to get her first pumpkin spice latte of the season. Shortly after her funeral her parents honored her request and they went to Starbuck's and they paid for several pumpkin spice lattes. Their only request was that when somebody requested a pumpkin spice latte it would be provided to them in a cup that would have a message #AJO, Alyssa's initials, which lead to her memorial page. They also put a video out on social media explaining why they did what they were doing and within hours it went viral. This random act of kindness in their daughter's memory would reach as far as Australia. There were pictures coming in from all over the world of people holding up signs that had the same message, #AJO. People everywhere were paying it forward in memory of a girl whose heart was the size of Texas.

Within days there were billboards going up around the country. National news outlets were talking about it, as well as people like Ellen DeGeneres and professional athletes. It was far more than a ripple effect, it was a pure tidal wave of generosity. Just as I mentioned earlier in the chapter, when you give, it comes back tenfold. The National TV show *Inside Edition* flew to Erie and did a feature story about this wave of giving that touched the hearts and lives of people everywhere.

I like to refer to what the O'Neills did as the ultimate "pay it forward". They took their family tragedy and their grief, and they turned it into the most incredibly positive movement that I've seen in my lifetime. Because of the number of offers to help and the contributions that were coming back to them, they eventually started the AJO Forever Foundation.

Through a combination of merchandise sales, fundraisers and continual donations, they are now helping other families who are faced with the same diagnosis. They are able to help with travel expenses as well as provide low-cost to no-cost epilepsy monitors to people who otherwise couldn't afford them. Twice annually they provide grants or service animals and they also provide thousands of dollars in scholarship funds to aspiring nurses. I encourage you to go to their website, AJOforever.com and learn more about the ultimate "pay it forward".

It shouldn't be a surprise to you that of course my favorite movie is *Pay It Forward*. I often think about what a wonderful world we'd have if we all did what the young character in the movie suggested. If each of us are on a mission to provide three random acts of kindness and in exchange simply ask people to do the same, we can create that ripple effect of kindness.

The smallest random act of kindness could change somebody's circumstances that day for the better. When you pay it forward you realize that life isn't just about you. Paying it forward can become an addiction, but what an addiction to have.

Generosity does not always have to be linked to money. Allowing somebody who has fewer items than you to cut in front of you in the grocery store is being generous. Even helping somebody load the groceries into their car is another form of generosity. Have you ever had a time when you received exceptional customer service? Imagine how happy you'd make that staff member if you took the time to tell their manager?

And this may even sound silly for a moment, but consider smiling at a stranger, because that may just change the entire direction of their day and yours. The possibilities are endless, but I guarantee that if you make a daily conscious effort of the simplest action that will add value to somebody else's life, you will have tenfold returns.

About the Author

onna Rae is the youngest of nine children, raised on a fruit farm in Western Pennsylvania.

After only one year in college, she dropped out and married at twenty years old. Shortly after, she and her husband purchased his family business. Donna Rae was working two jobs and raising two sons by the time she was twenty-seven. After purchasing another business, she and her business-partner husband felt the pressure of balancing home and business, and were amicably divorced. Donna Rae ran two businesses, raised two sons and was very involved with her community. She went on to purchase another business and also ran for political office.

Later, Donna Rae was diagnosed with degenerative disc disease, and then interstitial lung disease. She fought through chronic pain for many years before her first spinal surgery. Ten years and six spinal surgeries later, two neurosurgeons advised that her life as she knew it was over. She made the decision to sell her shares of the family business to her sons and move to Florida where she could continue her treatments.

Not one to take it all lying down, Donna Rae enrolled in a course for Motivational Speaking and Corporate Coaching, where she stumbled across her favorite speaker of all time, Mr. Les Brown. She grabbed the opportunity to train with her greatest mentor!

After losing two sisters tragically in 2017, Donna Rae sunk into a deep depression, before remembering the words that she reads in *The Secret* each day. THOUGHTS BECOME THINGS! Life was hard enough with chronic pain, but now she knew an even greater pain, the loss of two sisters. Despite that, Donna Rae attributes all the amazing things that happen in her life to the sincere gratitude that she has each morning when she plants her two feet on the floor.

At the time of this book edit, Donna Rae has learned that her lung disease has progressed and she will be put on the lung transplant list. With tremendous support from her sons, some great friends and family, she intends to prove that this is just another obstacle that will be the topic of her next book. She's not done living!

Web: www.donnaraeinspires.com
Email: donnaraeinspires@gmail.com
Facebook: Donna Rae
Instagram: Donna_Rae_Inspires
Youtube: Donna Rae